GET UP AND RIDE - THE CAMINO DE SANTIAGO

A CYCLING ADVENTURE STORY

JIM SHEA

CASUS
PUBLISHING

For Katie, who always keeps me on the right path, headed in the right direction.

Get Up and Ride

Asturias

Santiago
de Compostela

Finisterre

Galicia

Arzua

Sarria

Villafranca

Cruz de Ferro

Astor

Portugal

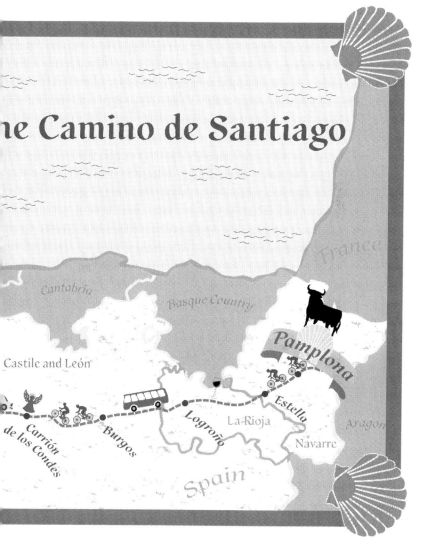

he Camino de Santiago

CONTENTS

PROLOGUE

I am not a professional writer. I'm not even much of a reader. And I am certainly not what most people would call a "cyclist." So how did I end up writing books about cycling?

I owe it to my brother-in-law, Marty. He has a way of getting me to do things. Things I would never consider doing. Things that are far outside of my comfort zone. Not by directly telling me to do them, but by suggesting that these things are, indeed, possible.

How would I describe Marty? Think of him as a burly, stocky version of Kramer from Seinfeld. He is effortlessly comical and is a magnet for hilarity. Crazy and funny stories seem to follow him wherever he goes. And that's why you want to be with him as much as possible.

Marty is an artist and former inner-city public school art teacher. He is also an avid cyclist. In 2010, he convinced me to join him on a 340-mile bike ride from Pittsburgh, PA to Washington, DC along the Great Allegheny Passage and C&O Canal trails. I didn't even own a bicycle and had never ridden more than 25 miles in one day. As an engineer and workaholic executive, I wasn't the least bit interested in spending one of my two weeks of vacation sitting on a hard saddle, inhaling bugs and dodging thunderstorms on a muddy trail.

But he kept bringing it up. He said that being in the woods would help clear my mind. He said it would be an adventure. He said we'd make memories together. Finally, I relented and agreed to the trip.

When I asked Marty what we'd be doing every day, he simply said:

"We're just gonna get up and ride. What more do you need to know?"

But I needed to know. I wanted specifics, like how many miles we'd ride each day, where we'd stay, what we'd need to bring, and what dangerous creatures we might encounter along the way.

"*Why don't you see what you can do?*" Marty responded.

In that moment, I realized that if any planning was going to happen, it was up to me. I sprang into action, planned the trip, and trained extensively. Several months later, in August 2010, we completed the five-day ride together.

And what a ride it was. Each day on the trail, we had chance encounters with locals and other characters that amazed us and kept us laughing.

A year after the trip, during our annual beach vacation, Marty proposed something else outside of my comfort zone. He said "we" should write a book about it.

"A book?" I asked. "I don't think there's enough material for a book. Plus, remember? I don't even read books."

"I really think there's a book here," said Marty confidently. "*Why don't you see what you can do?*"

There was that phrase again. That afternoon, while still on vacation, I opened my laptop and began writing some stories from the trip. I wrote little bits here and there—on weekends, vacations, and business trips.

Over the next nine years, it took shape. My wife (Katie), my mother (Phyllis), and Marty's wife (Belle) helped with the editing. Belle would read chapters aloud to Marty as I'd finish them. But it was still a long way from being a book.

At Thanksgiving 2020, as Katie and Belle put away the last of the leftovers, Marty and I sat around the fire pit in his backyard and chatted about all sorts of inane things.

"Jumbo, I have no idea what I'm going to get my biking friends for Christmas," he said. "Do you think it would be possible to get that book done in time so I could give out copies by then?"

"I don't know, Marty. There's still a ton to do. I need to finish the writing, get it proofread, and design a cover. Then I need to figure out how to actually publish a book."

"*Why don't you see what you can do?*" said Marty, predictably.

For the next three weeks, I worked on it from 4:00 to 8:00 a.m., at which time I'd begin my normal ten-hour workday. At around 6:00 p.m., I would get back to the book until I collapsed, typically around midnight. On December 10th, 2020, it was ready. I called Marty.

"Hey Marty, it's finished. I'm getting ready to hit the 'publish' button. Are you okay with everything I wrote? There's a lot of really personal stuff about you in here, and you've never actually read it."

"Yeah, Belle has read most of it to me. I'm good with it. Go for it!"

I hit the button, and on December 11th, 2020, the first "Get Up and Ride" book was born.

And two weeks later, on Christmas Day, Marty finally sat down and read it.

IF WE THOUGHT that doing the ride and writing the book was fun, we had no idea how much joy the next few years would bring, as thousands of folks around the world shared in our story. Many have told us that the book inspired them to "get up and ride" these trails themselves. Perhaps you're one of them.

What seems to have resonated the most with our readers— even more than the biking adventure—is the authentic friend- ship Marty and I share. I can tell you that, after knowing him for 40 years, we have just as much fun together now as we did when we were in our twenties.

With that in mind, in 2023—in our sixties, retired, and well past the halfway mark in our lives—we decided we were overdue for a new adventure. Something big. Something outside of our comfort zone. And something that would give us the opportunity to reflect on how to spend whatever time we might have left on this planet.

That is what this book is about. Come along with us for the ride. It may take you outside of your comfort zone, too, even if you never leave your couch.

1

SOMETHING TO DO

"What are the metrics on this account?"

The operations director was digging for answers. The account manager quickly scanned her computer for the figures.

"Overall satisfaction score is 89.5," she replied. "Utilization score is 93..."

Sitting in my home office in February 2023, on my fifth straight hour of Zoom meetings, I daydreamed. This was a full-day account review, attended remotely by over 80 people whose faces were framed in tiny squares, spread across four screens on my computer. I am 100% sure that at least 50% of them were daydreaming too.

"... total number of users is up twelve percent over last year..."

I was daydreaming about biking. Specifically, about going on a long bike trip. A trip with a certain "character"—my brother-in-law, Marty.

Marty and I had cycled the 340-mile Great Allegheny Passage (GAP) and C&O Canal trails from Pittsburgh, PA to Washington, DC several times. Since our last ride in 2019, we'd been talking about finding a new trail for our next adventure, and I'd started looking at the Erie Canal path across Upstate New York. It was time to plan if we were going to make it happen that summer.

I had another reason to be daydreaming. I was retiring in two months. After working in corporate America for nearly 40 years, I was "hanging up my cleats." And exchanging them for a different kind of cleats—the kind that clip into bike pedals.

Just then, I had a thought. I don't really know where it came from. It was a bolt from the blue. But it seemed like a pretty good thought, and maybe a great one. So good, in fact, that I felt a sense of urgency in sharing it.

I muted my computer's microphone and turned off the camera. I stood up, walked out of the room, down the hallway and into the bathroom, and called Marty.

~

TO UNDERSTAND this book and appreciate this story, it's helpful to have some understanding of Marty and the relationship he and I share. Please bear with me for a bit of background.

Marty and I have known each other for over four decades. I grew up in an affluent suburb in the Washington, DC area; Marty is from a blue-collar section of Philadelphia. He's an artist and retired art teacher who goes with the flow; I'm an engineer and retired corporate executive who plans out everything I do.

Our lives intersected in 1984 when we met—and eventually married—two sisters from the Pittsburgh area. Marty and Belle settled in Pittsburgh, and Katie and I ended up in Pittsburgh fifteen years later by way of San Francisco and Maryland. Both families raised three sons—all of similar ages. As in most families, our children call me "Dad." Marty's children call him "Marty."

Marty's favorite activity is sitting. Years ago, Katie used one of Newton's Laws to describe him: *A Marty at rest tends to stay at rest; a Marty in motion will soon be at rest.*

Marty knows chairs like no one else. I'm talking about the details of chairs, like the material of the cushions, the precise angle of the back of a chair, and a chair's ability to swivel or rock. He is also keenly aware of the presence (or absence) of chairs in a room, as well as the specific placement of those chairs.

For me, however, chairs are not a top priority, as I'm always moving and rarely sit. One summer, our families shared a beach house in North Carolina's Outer Banks, and Marty stepped into our bedroom at the end of the week.

"Jumbo, where is your chair?"

"Chair?" I looked around. "I guess there isn't one in here. You and Belle have one in your room?"

"Of course. I've been sitting in it all week." Marty looked at me quizzically. "You mean... you never had the urge to sit down in your room this past week? Not even once?"

"Well, sure, when I put my shoes on, I sit on the edge of the bed here for a minute. Then I get up and leave the room."

"Sheesh, Jumbo, you need to chill a little more."

After observing the two of us at the beach, our Chinese sister-in-law, Xiao Hong, gave Marty the name "Bu Dong," which means "not moving." And she gave me the name "Duo Dong," which means "much moving." I like to be active, while Marty has perfected the art of being inactive.

The puzzling thing is that although Marty doesn't like to move, he rides his bike nearly every day. In fact, he rode over 4,000 miles last year. This is probably because biking is one of the few forms of exercise one can perform while sitting.

Marty is 6'1", 220 pounds and 65 years old. I am 5'8", 160 pounds and just turned 60. We are very different people whose paths would never have crossed had we not married two sisters.

But we have developed a deep friendship over the years, a core element of which is inane banter about things of little interest to other people.

One important aspect of our relationship is how we work together to accomplish tasks, particularly the planning of trips. It typically goes something like this.

Marty and I discuss doing something together, with the idea usually initiated by Marty. After he throws out the concept, I think about it. Then I get excited about it. Finally, I come back to Marty and say we should do it. He responds and says "we" should start doing some planning. Of course, I agree.

And then Marty says, "Jumbo, *why don't you see what you can do?*"

From there, I spring into action and plan the entire trip. I buy guidebooks and spend days performing detailed research. I study the history of the towns, analyze weather patterns, calculate distance and elevation, identify places to stay, and put together spreadsheets. And that's precisely the way it worked with our first GAP/C&O trip in 2010.

"*See what you can do*" may sound like a casual, nonchalant expression. But let me tell you, it gets results. I can't control myself. When I hear that phrase, I turn into a whirling dervish on a singular mission.

And Marty knows this. Therefore, he uses this phrase selectively and judiciously. He refers to his invoking of this expression as "punching in the codes," as a president might do when sending nuclear missiles across the ocean with no way to reclaim them. It's an action that has consequences, and it can't be undone.

The good thing is that Marty is always happy with whatever plan I come up with. He never criticizes it and rarely suggests any changes. It's a symbiotic relationship.

∾

BACK TO FEBRUARY 2023. With my computer squawking away in the other room, I dialed Marty. He immediately answered.

"Character here, can I help you?" Marty feigned a businesslike tone, with a hint of his Philly accent still noticeable despite having lived in Pittsburgh for 45 years.

"Is this *the* character? The guy from that book 'Get Up and Ride?'" I played along.

"Yeah, you got him. Is this the author? That guy who writes humorous true stories, mostly about me?"

"Yup, that's me."

Marty then broke out of "character" and converted to his usual jovial self. "Yo, Jumbo, whassup?"

"Hey Marty, what are you doing?" He had been retired for a year at this point, so he was typically in "super-chill" mode.

"What am I doing? I'm talking to you."

I shook my head and chuckled. "I meant before that."

"Oh, before that?" Marty thought for few seconds. "Nothing."

"Nothing?"

"Yeah, I had nothing to do. But now I have something to do. I'm talking to you."

"It's nice to have something to do, isn't it?"

"Jumbo, that's what retirement is all about. You're always looking for something to do. And once you find it, and you do it, you're back to having nothing to do. And then you start looking for something to do all over again."

"Can't wait."

"How 'bout you Jumbo? What are you up to today?"

"Working. I'm on a Zoom right now. Just stepped out." I could still hear the account reviews on the call I had abandoned in the other room. I wondered if they missed me.

"You still dealing with that thing?" Marty asked.

"That *thing*?"

"Yeah, that *job* thing, Jumbo. That thing is a serious

nuisance. It's always getting in the way of us doing stuff together."

"Yeah, but come April, I'll be like you."

"You know, I've been thinking about that. I'm not sure if you can handle this, Jumbo. You're always so active. I'm not sure you're built for this."

"Well, I'm gonna give it a try," I said. "That's why I'm calling. I got an idea. Something to do. It's big."

"Yeah, whaddya got?"

"Well, you know how we were talking about a bike trip this summer?"

"Yeah, we need one, Jumbo."

"And remember how we were talking about riding the Erie Canal?"

"Yeah."

"Well, I've been thinking. The Erie Canal sounds great, and we gotta do that at some point. But I had another idea. And when I think about it, I get pretty excited."

"Lay it on me."

"Camino."

"Huh?"

"Camino de Santiago. The Way of St. James—in Spain."

"Whoa—isn't that the month-long pilgrimage walk people do? The Martin Sheen movie, right?"

"Yeah. But I think we can bike it. I remember seeing some guys on bikes in the movie."

"How long?"

"Not sure, probably ten to twelve days. The whole thing is about 500 miles across northern Spain."

"What kind of trails? What kind of bikes?" Marty was asking for details. I could tell he was interested.

"I need to do some more research, but probably mountain bikes."

"Sounds like an adventure. And a great way to start your

retirement. Plus, it would give me something to do for almost two weeks."

"Does it get your blood pumping, thinking about it?" Marty's resting heart rate is normally around 40 beats per minute—the result of a life without stress and daily four-hour bike rides.

"Gotta tell you Jumbo, I'm excited. I think my heart rate's up to about forty-five."

"Good. Me too. *So...*" I baited him.

"What?"

"Should I... you know..."

"Oh, got it Jumbo," Marty recognized what I was asking him to do. *"Why don't you see what you can do?"*

"Really? Are you *actually* telling me to 'see what I can do?' Today? Right now? For a bike trip on the Camino?"

"Yes, Jumbo, take this as your official '*see what you can do.*'"

It is noteworthy that in this case, the trip was initially my idea, and I lured Marty into giving me the order to plan it. But it didn't matter—his words were all I needed to hear. The planning process began that day, the genesis of a cycling odyssey that would take us across the width of Spain using (mostly) the power of our own two legs.

2

THE CAMINO DE SANTIAGO

Once I had been given (or, rather, had given myself) my marching orders, the first task was to learn more about the Camino. Neither Marty nor I spoke any Spanish, so the language barrier had the potential to be an issue. However, lots of information was available in English, so I dove in and started doing some research. Stay with me—this is (by far) the longest history lesson in the book. If you can make it through the next few pages, you're home free.

Camino is the Spanish word for "Way," and *Santiago* means "St. James." James (the Greater) was one of Jesus' twelve apostles and was part of a family of fishermen, the son of Zebedee and brother of John the Evangelist (i.e., Gospel writer). Jesus called James and John to join him at the shore of the Sea of Galilee in Israel, and they were by his side throughout his public ministry.

After Jesus died in 33 AD, the apostles fanned out all over, preaching the message of Christianity. James went to Spain and later returned to Jerusalem, where he was beheaded by King Herod II in 44 AD.

No one really knew what happened to James' body for over

800 years. However, one evening in the ninth century, in an area in northwestern Spain called Galicia, a shepherd named Pelagius "the Hermit" saw a bright light in the sky and heard some odd sounds coming from the woods. He reported it to the local bishop, who rounded up several others and headed out to the site. They cleared the shrubs, dug around, and, to their amazement, discovered three tombs. The bishop declared that the remains in the central tomb belonged to St. James, and the other two were attributed to James' primary disciples—Athanasius and Theodore.

How did St. James' body get from Jerusalem to Spain? This is where legend, fact, and mystery become intertwined. Tradition holds that after James' death, his body was transported from Israel to Galicia in a boat by these two disciples, who were led by angels. They then buried him in this location inland from the coast, and were later entombed there themselves.

In the Middle Ages, many religious sites in Europe were collecting important relics and building churches to house them, hoping pilgrims would come visit. Jerusalem had Jesus, Rome had St. Peter, and now, it seemed, Spain had St. James. The king of that region (Alphonso II) got wind of the discovery and—recognizing the importance and potential—built a small chapel above the tombs. Later, he commissioned a larger church hoping to create a pilgrimage site, in what is today the city of Santiago de Compostela.

King Alphonso II was successful in achieving his goal. His successor, Alphonso III, built an even larger church there, which was burned by the Moors and then replaced with the current Cathedral of Santiago de Compostela, consecrated in 1211. This Romanesque temple has become a destination for millions of pilgrims over the centuries, all paying homage to St. James.

In the Middle Ages, pilgrims would leave from their hometowns from all over Europe, typically in groups, and make their way to Santiago de Compostela. As a result, many Camino routes developed, all leading to Santiago. The scallop shell, often found on the shores of Galicia, has become the symbol of the Camino. Its lines are said to represent the different paths which converge at the burial site of St. James. Early pilgrims customarily carried back a Galician scallop shell upon returning from Santiago as proof of completing their journey. Today, pilgrims attach a shell to their backpacks as a way of identifying themselves.

Camino marker with scallop symbol

Besides the religious aspect, the early kings soon realized the Camino brought another benefit to the region. Spain had been fending off attacks by the Moors for centuries. The influx of pilgrims coming from all over Europe to travel across northern Spain—some of them settling there—resulted in a growing Christian population. This was a deterrent to the

Moors, who knew not to pick fights when they were outnumbered. In fact, the Spanish kings offered incentives to encourage people to settle along the routes, and some of the small towns grew into cities and thriving communities.

Are you still with me? Or did you nod off? It happens to me, too. Hang in there—just a few more pages of history and I'll get back to the story.

Some of the earliest pilgrims walked the Camino del Norte —along the northern coastline of Spain—and the Camino Primitivo, which starts near the north coast in Oviedo and cuts inland to Santiago. King Alfonso II himself made one of the initial pilgrimages in the ninth century following these routes.

Another popular path is the Camino Portuguese, which starts in Lisbon and heads up the coast of Portugal. Many also walk the Camino Inglés, which begins in the Spanish city of Ferrol, directly north of Santiago.

But the most well-known and well-traveled route is the Camino Francés, or "French Way." When I first heard the name, I envisioned that biking "the French Way" would involve nibbling on croissants and sipping wine as we pedaled across the countryside. However, I later learned that this route earned its name from the fact that—although over 90% of it is in Spain —it originates on the French side of the Pyrenees, in the village of St. Jean Pied de Port (which, aptly, means "St. John Foot Port").

The Camino Francés was developed in the 11th century. Following an old Roman trade route, it makes its way over the Pyrenees, across northern Spain, and ultimately to Santiago. This 490-mile path is traveled by about half of all Camino pilgrims and is the route used in the movie "The Way," a 2010 film starring Martin Sheen. In the movie, Sheen's character, Tom, loses his son on the Camino Francés and walks the trail in his honor, carrying his ashes with him. Marty and I had seen the movie with Belle and Katie a few years after its release.

I suggested to Marty that we follow the Camino Francés for our trip. Knowing nothing about it, except for what he vaguely recalled from the movie, he immediately and enthusiastically agreed.

The Camino Francés is structured so that there are towns approximately twelve to fifteen miles apart, about the distance a person can walk in a day with a heavy backpack. On average, it takes about five weeks to complete the pilgrimage on foot. To support pilgrims in the Middle Ages, local kings and clergy built hospitals, bridges, monasteries, and hostels in these towns, many of which still stand.

As I read more about the Camino, I learned that the path actually has an ancient history which pre-dates the discovery of St. James' body. As early as 1000 BC, pagan Celtic/Iberian tribes would make pilgrimages to their gods from the interior of Spain (then called "Iberia") to the Atlantic Coast about 50 miles west of the city of Santiago. They would end at Cape Finisterre at what is now the town of Fisterra, which translates to "end of the earth." Watching the sun set over the ocean was a spiritual experience for them, and they would offer prayers to their gods at this spot.

By 200 BC, the Romans occupied Iberia and built roads and other infrastructure, including some roads used by pilgrims today. When the Romans reached Finisterre, they also believed they had found the end of the world, as this was the farthest west their empire had ever been. Today, some pilgrims spend an extra three or four days and walk from Santiago to Cape Finisterre (or nearby Muxia) to take in the view of the rocky coastline.

Among Christians, the pilgrimage to Santiago continued to rise in popularity and reached a peak in the 12th and 13th centuries, with over 250,000 pilgrims making the journey each year. Without the internet, TV, and social media, how could this have happened?

First, in the 12th century, Pope Callixtus II, a big fan of the Camino, published the first-ever guidebook for the French Way. Unfortunately, he didn't include any tips for bikers, so I decided not to buy a copy before our trip.

Second, Catholic pilgrims were offered an indulgence (promising reduced time in purgatory) by walking the Camino, so it became a way of paying a penance. The bigger the sin, the longer the walk. Evidently, a lot of sinning was going on in those days, as lots of people would work off their transgressions by trekking across Spain.

Third, pilgrimages were sometimes imposed by judges as a sentence for a crime. In Belgium, a tradition still holds whereby one prisoner is pardoned and released each year (a modern day "We-want-Barabbas") under the condition that, accompanied by a guard, the criminal walks to Santiago wearing a heavy backpack. And in the Middle Ages, wealthy citizens who were ordered to serve a sentence would sometimes *pay* pilgrims to hike the Camino on their behalf. I guess money can buy just about anything.

Then, starting in the 14th century, things took a turn, and the Camino experienced a precipitous decline. The most obvious reason was the Black Death plague, which wiped out nearly half of Europe's population in the mid-1300s. Not surprisingly, walking the Camino was low on the priority list.

But there were other factors. In the early 1500s, a German monk, Martin Luther, published a series of teachings which criticized practices of the Catholic church, including two elements that were central to the Camino—venerating relics and granting indulgences. This sparked the Protestant Reformation, which spread quickly across Europe, further reducing the number of Catholic pilgrims on the Camino.

The Reformation led to a series of religious wars, including the 1595 Holy War between France and Spain. In the 1600s, Louis XIV of France forbade citizens from traveling to Santiago in order to stop trade with Spain. The number of pilgrims declined to just a few hundred per year and remained that way for centuries.

Then, just 40 years ago in the 1980s, Dr. Elias Valiña Sampedro, a priest from the Camino town of O Cebreiro, took it upon himself to bring back the forgotten Camino. He had written his thesis on the Way, having studied it for years. He realized that over centuries of minimal usage, the trail had fallen into disrepair and even lacked basic signage to enable pilgrims to easily follow it.

So, Valiña grabbed a few cans of yellow paint left over from some recent roadwork and began marking the Camino Francés using arrows, now known as "waymarks." One day, while painting yellow pointers in the Pyrenees, some local police spotted him, assumed he was a vandal, and hauled him into the station. Valiña explained himself and was released. He continued to work tirelessly over the next few years with local parishes and governments to improve the path and open pilgrim *albergues* (hostels). He died in 1989 at the age of 60.

Largely because of Valiña's work, over the next 25 years, the Camino saw a steady increase in pilgrims—from only 1,250 in 1985 to 100,000 in 1993 to 270,000 in 2010. Then, the release of "The Way" in 2010 kicked things into an even higher gear, especially with Americans: by 2022, over 400,000 pilgrims arrived in Santiago. We are now amid the largest expansion in Camino usage in history. Many still do it for spiritual reasons, but increasingly people seek it as a "bucket list" adventure.

Marty and I would clearly have lots of company on the Camino in 2023. I felt sure this would make for some memorable chance encounters with genuine characters (in addition to Marty).

3

SPREADSHEETS

After learning about the history of the Camino, I began looking into the Camino Francés route in more detail. Only five percent of pilgrims travel on bikes, so far less information was available than if we were walking. However, I found a few websites, as well as a book entitled "Cycling the Camino de Santiago," by Mike Wells, which proved quite helpful.

I assessed potential starting points and mapped out the distance and elevation gain between towns. Our past GAP/C&O biking adventures had been relatively flat, so hills had not been a factor. In fact, the total elevation gain on those trips had been less than 2,500 feet over the entire 340 miles. On the French Way, if we started in St. Jean Pied de Port, we would climb nearly 30,000 feet over 490 miles. Between St. Jean and Pamplona alone, the ascent would be 5,000 feet over just 40 miles. Were we crazy to attempt this?

Realizing we were in for a challenging ride, I wanted to make sure we could make it to each town without being completely wiped out by the end of the day. So I thought it made sense to plan longer distances on days with less climbing and shorter distances on days with more hills.

Compared to those traveling the Camino on foot, we could cover more ground each day—perhaps two or three times the distance. But we didn't want to just blow through the trip; we wanted to have time to see the towns, interact with people, and even get off our bikes and hike with other pilgrims occasionally. I'd read that walkers end up traveling with some of the same people for several days and often develop lifelong friendships. We would not have the same opportunity on two wheels, but we wanted to leave ourselves open to possibilities.

I had another reason to want to take it at a slower pace than our past trips. As a lifelong Catholic, I was drawn to the Camino for religious reasons. I wanted to spend time in the churches and experience what millions of other Christians had encountered over the centuries. Also, St. James is my patron saint, and I looked forward to visiting his final resting place.

Marty, on the other hand, is not religious. He was primarily interested in a fun biking adventure, as well as in the history, scenery, and people we'd come across in Spain. However, Marty is somewhat of an enigma. While he is certainly jovial and lighthearted, Marty is also a deeply reflective and thoughtful person and often uses his long rides to process things. I knew he would also appreciate the spiritual aspect of the Camino.

I put together an Excel spreadsheet with three alternate itineraries—of ten, eleven, and twelve days. Each itinerary listed the towns we would visit, where we would stay, the distances and elevation gains between towns, and the primary points of interest.

We met Marty and Belle at a restaurant the following Sunday for dinner. I printed off copies of the itineraries and presented them to Marty.

At first, he didn't know what he was looking at, mainly because he can't see. Well, that's a bit of an exaggeration, but without reading glasses, Marty couldn't read a children's book with 30-point font. I refer to his eyesight as one of his two "physical frailties"—not bad for a guy who's 65. You will learn about his other challenge later on.

At this point, I'm sure you're wondering why Marty calls me "Jumbo." This odd moniker actually owes itself to Marty's poor eyesight, not my physical stature. Years ago, when Marty added me as a contact in his cell phone, instead of typing "Jimbo," he accidentally typed "Jumbo." His phone was paired with his car, and when I would call him, his dashboard read: *"Call from... Jumbo."* He got such a kick out of it that he never changed it. The name stuck.

Even though Marty can't read without glasses, for some reason he never has a pair handy when he needs them. Seeing Marty squinting at the paper, Katie pulled out her reading glasses and handed them to him. Marty focused on one of the three spreadsheet pages I'd printed. He was speechless.

"Jumbo, holy cow, this is amazing!"

"Well, you did use *the phrase*, you know."

"I know, but... *you did all this in the last four days?*"

"Yeah, whaddya think?"

"I couldn't do this if you gave me a month."

"That's the ten-day itinerary you're looking at. Those other pages have two other options—eleven and twelve days."

Marty flipped to the other pages.

"Jumbo, this is some serious 'seeing what you can do.'"

"Do you have a preference on how many days—which itinerary?"

"Well, you know I tend to be pretty flexible," Marty grinned. "And without something like this, you know what my typical approach would be for each day, right?"

"What?"

"Get up and ride."

"Oh yeah. Well, I actually thought about just doing that. But with nearly half a million people on the Camino this year, I'm thinking we should make hotel reservations."

I had done some research on lodging and had actually spoken with a friend of a friend, Jeanette, who had completed the Camino Francés the previous year. Most pilgrims stay in albergues, which are like hostels, similar to the places depicted in "The Way." Some albergues take reservations, but others do not. Also, they often give priority to walkers over cyclists, the theory being that if there is "no room at the inn," bikers can more easily make their way to the next town to find a bed.

Jeanette had told me about her albergue experience. People are coming and going at all hours, beds are creaking, and a cacophony of snoring, coughing, and farting continues throughout the night. She said she didn't sleep for a month.

I explained all this to Marty, and we agreed we would stay in hotels and Airbnbs. While we would miss out on the social aspect of the dorm-style accommodations, we'd still have many other opportunities to spend time with pilgrims—on the trail, in cafés, and at dinners. And we didn't think we should be trying to dodge pilgrims on our bikes in a sleep-deprived stupor.

"When should we go?" asked Marty.

"I'm thinking September. The weather should still be good, and the crowds will be down a bit. Also it will give us—well, really, me—more time to train, since I haven't been on the bike since last September."

I looked at Belle, who—in addition to being Marty's wife—functions as Marty's calendar.

"September works. Marty's free," she said.

"Well, Jumbo, nice work on this," said Marty.

"You want to look at the itineraries and the towns and stuff? Any preference on which hotels or where in town you'd want to stay?"

"I'm good with anything. I trust you. Surprise me."

Planning is certainly easier when you don't need to get approval from the person with whom you're traveling.

During dinner, we asked Belle and Katie if they wanted to join us for some traveling in Spain, either before or after our journey. They politely declined, saying they preferred to go another time on a dedicated trip where we could spend more time together.

We finished our dinner and headed out of the restaurant. Near the exit we passed a raw bar, where oysters, scallops, and shrimp were buried in a large case full of ice. At one end were several large, white scallop shells.

Marty got the attention of the man behind the counter. "Excuse me, would it be possible for us to get two of those shells?"

"Sure, what for?" he replied.

"We'd like to take them with us on the Camino de Santiago."

The man raised his eyebrows. Shrugging his shoulders, he pulled two shells out of the ice, dried them off, and handed them to us.

I'm certain these would become the most well-traveled scallop shells ever to leave that raw bar.

THE NEXT DAY, I looked over the spreadsheets and settled on the eleven-day itinerary. Ideally, we would start in St. Jean Pied de Port, on the French side of the Pyrenees, but in looking at airports and transportation options, it seemed like it would be best to start in Pamplona. This would cut off the first 40 miles —the most challenging section—but would make things easier logistically.

I scheduled flights into Pamplona and out of Santiago de Compostela, arranging for two nights in Pamplona and two in Santiago. On the front end, this would give us time to work off jet lag and a buffer in case there were issues with our flights. On the back end, we would have time to explore Santiago and experience Mass at the cathedral on a Sunday. Also, our cousin-in-law and close friend, Pat, was planning to do some traveling in Portugal around that time and offered to meet us at the end of our trip to celebrate.

Our itinerary would have us staying in twelve towns—Pamplona, Estella, Logroño, Belorado, Burgos, Carrión de los Condes, León, Astorga, Villafranca del Bierzo, Sarria, Arzua and Santiago de Compostela.

I booked accommodations for us in each of the towns. Step one was complete. I guess we were really doing this.

4

THE "OLD ME"

A few weeks later, as my 60th birthday approached, it occurred to me that my current body was not the same as the one that had completed the initial GAP/C&O ride with Marty thirteen years earlier. In fact, it had already been four years since our last Pittsburgh-to-DC trip in 2019. I was wondering how I would be able to handle such a challenging journey.

On a Wednesday in March, I went to Walgreens to pick up some toiletries. I approached the checkout counter, set down my basket, and the clerk began scanning my items.

"Should'a come in yesterday," she said.

"Why?"

"Senior day. First Tuesday of every month. Seniors get twenty percent off."

Seniors? Seriously?

"Darn, I just missed it," I replied. "What's the age requirement?"

"Sixty."

"Great—thanks. In two months, I'll qualify!"

She rang up the total, without any recognition of her faux pas.

About a month later, I started having some lower back pain, which had been a recurring issue for me over the past few years. With this big trip coming up, and the training required, I decided to see a chiropractor for the first time.

During the initial visit, I handed my insurance card to the woman at the front desk. She then introduced me to the doctor, who took some X-rays and checked me out. Afterwards, he sat me down in his office.

"Mr. Shea, you have some thinning in the L5 disc, and it's restricting your range of motion in the L3 and L4," he said, pointing at the X-ray. "I recommend a course of therapy that should be able to reduce the pain and get you on a path to a healthier spine in a few months."

"That's good to hear. I'm actually planning a long cycling trip in Spain in September. You think I can get my back in shape to handle it by then?"

"I do. By the way, it also looks like you may have some loss of bone mass. You should get that checked out with a DXA scan at some point."

"Okay."

"Now, most of what we do here isn't covered by insurance," said the doctor. "There will end up being a fair amount out of pocket."

"That's alright, I need to do this."

"We'll run the numbers and give you the estimated total when you leave. First, let's get you going with some therapy."

I completed several exercises, sat on a spine-stretching vibrating chair, and got "adjusted" on the table—a series of neck and back cracks that promised to make me feel better.

On my way out, I met the doctor at the front desk.

"Nice start, Mr. Shea. We'll set you up to come back next Monday. Oh, and about the insurance. I was wrong—I assumed you were on Medicare. Since you're still on private insurance, the out-of-pocket cost won't be as much as I thought."

I looked at him in dismay. *Medicare?* I could accept the fact that Walgreens had aged me by two months, but *five years?*

With reminders of my advancing age coming with increasing frequency, I was struck by two thoughts. First, if we were going to do a trip like this, we'd better do it now. At the rate I was going, the next time I shopped at Walgreens I might be offered the octogenarian's discount and a special parking space.

Second, I needed to train extensively. The Camino would be a much more difficult ride than our past rail-trail trips and would require us to be in even better condition. On our previous excursions, we were on wide, flat, well-groomed paths using bikes with narrow tires. The Camino would involve riding the pilgrim's hiking path for significant stretches—with rocks, mud, and lots of climbing. We would need to use mountain bikes with wide, knobby tires. As a sporadic cyclist with a thinning L5, I was a bit intimidated. It was time to log some miles.

5

THE "NEW ME"

In April, I retired from my job. On my first day of retirement, Marty and I took a 40-mile ride on our local bike path—the Montour Trail—at noon on a beautiful, sunny Monday.

It was springtime in Pittsburgh, and green shoots were popping everywhere. The yellow forsythia blossoms were on their way out, replaced by the magenta tentacles of redbud trees. The stream alongside the path was running fast, carrying the spring rains to their final destination—the Ohio River. We had the trail nearly to ourselves.

After we'd ridden twenty miles, we stopped to take a break before turning around. We parked our bikes and walked over to a covered deck, with two benches facing each other. Marty took one bench, and I took the other. I sucked on my water bottle.

We talked about retirement, my new granddaughter, and what we'd had for breakfast. Adhering to the "ten mile rule*,"

---

* Marty is not a big "rules" person. However, one of his few rules for biking is that you may not talk about food until you are within ten miles of finishing the ride. If you discuss food too early, he says, you will drive yourself crazy and will never finish the ride. With ten miles to go, starting to think and talk about food

we avoided any discussion of what we would eat after the ride. That would occur about halfway through the return trip.

"You know, Marty, we've been sitting here for what... ten or fifteen minutes, right? The 'old me' would have stood up by now and said something like 'okay, ready to head back?'"

"Yes!" exclaimed Marty. "That's *exactly* what the 'old you' would have said." He paused. "So... you're telling me you're *not* saying that?"

"Right. I'm not even standing up. See?"

"Nice, Jumbo. I like it." Marty nodded, taking in the scenery. He had absolutely no intention of leaving any time soon.

"Yup, the 'old me'—I'm putting him in a box, on the shelf." I pointed to the shelf adjacent to the bench and drew an outline of a box with my fingers.

"And this 'new you'—he just sits, right? No timetable?"

"Yup."

As I sat there, I began thinking about this new reality and how it would work in practice. Then, I got concerned.

"Marty, what happens if there's an urgent situation? Like... what if Katie calls while we're sitting here, saying she slipped and fell and hurt herself? I'll need to get the 'old me' off the shelf and bring him back, right?" I looked at the imaginary box on the shelf.

"No, Jumbo, that's not how you do it. The 'old you' is *history*," Marty said while pointing to the shelf. "The 'new you' can *accommodate* those types of situations. You need to incorporate these things into the 'new you.'"

"What?"

"Yeah, Jumbo, let me explain." He looked at me with a

---

will give you the energy to pick up the pace and finish strong. Since Marty has ridden tens of thousands of miles, he has had many hours to formulate and validate this rule. Who am I to argue with him?

serious expression. "So, this 'new you' you're becoming—this is basically what I've been my whole life, right?"

"Yes."

"So you know I have a lot of experience with this, right?"

"Of course."

"Okay, well, remember that big house fire we had ten years ago? There I was, in super-chill mode, sitting in my living room, reading a magazine. Suddenly, I got a call from my neighbor saying there were flames coming out of my attic window."

"Yeah, I remember that."

"What did I do? BOOM! I jumped up, called 911, grabbed the fire extinguisher, ran up the stairs, and started spraying."

"And later on, after the firemen put out the fire, you regained your chill?"

"Well, it took a while. I mean, remember? There was a lot of damage, and water was everywhere. We had to rent another place for six months while they fixed up our house."

"But ultimately, you're back to the way you were. Same Marty, just a temporary stressful situation."

"Exactly. The 'new you' can *accommodate* those situations. That's where you want to be, Jumbo."

I looked at the invisible "old me" on the shelf. This would take some time, but I could see the benefits, and I was up for the challenge. Now I needed to explain it to Katie.

6

TEST RIDE

We continued training during the summer, increasing our mileage and adding hills.

With one month to go, we began discussing what to bring, starting with the bikes. Although several companies offer bike rentals on the Camino, we decided we'd bring our own mountain bikes—for two reasons.

First, we wanted to make sure we would be comfortable with our equipment. Marty is very handy with bikes, so we felt he could address any repairs we'd need to make along the way.

Second, Marty has a deep personal relationship with his bikes, and he wanted to reward his beloved twelve-year-old Trek Paragon with a trip to Spain.

"Jumbo, just think, when we get back, every time you look at your bike hanging in your garage, it will thank you. And it'll bring back memories of our trip."

Next, we had to decide how to carry our gear. We settled on using a set of two waterproof panniers (saddlebags) which would attach to either side of a rear rack and would carry our clothing and supplies.

As far as clothes, we decided to bring three sets of bike

shorts and shirts, as well as a couple of T-shirts and shorts for evening wear. Since temperatures could range from 45 to 80 degrees during our trip, we also packed a long-sleeve pullover and long pants. We expected we would have some rain, so we brought a rain shell and a pair of shorts which claimed to be waterproof. As for shoes, we had clip-in mountain biking shoes that had good tread and would double as hiking shoes.

There were a lot of other odds and ends we needed to pack. I suggested to Marty that both of us didn't need to carry all the same things—we could divide and conquer. One day, at Marty's house, I presented a list covering what each of us would bring.

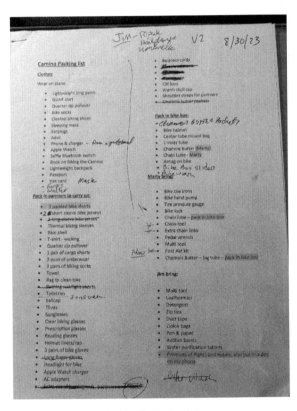

Packing list (by Jumbo)

"Jumbo, you've been retired for five months, but there's still a lot of the 'old you' left in there. Nice work."

"Thanks."

"Hey, there is one more thing we should bring."

"What?"

"Cigars. For our celebration at the end."

"Can't we just buy them over there?"

"We probably can, but I'll bet they won't be this nice."

Marty went into his kitchen, opened a drawer, and pulled out a box of cigars. He opened the lid—at least fifteen stogies remained. I immediately recognized them—they were high-end Cohibas, costing about $30 each.

"That's like a five or six hundred dollar box," I said. "Why do you have these? You hardly ever smoke cigars."

"Remember when I lost my credit card a few months ago?"

"Yeah."

"Well, some guy found it and started using it. He was buying some expensive stuff. By the time I realized it was gone and called the credit card company, he had already bought a big screen TV, a watch, and some jewelry. I wasn't responsible for any of it, thankfully."

"You're lucky."

"Yeah, so about two weeks later, I got this box in the mail from an online cigar company. It had a little card inside with a typed note that just said 'Thanks.'"

"What?!"

"I looked at my credit card bill, and there it was. It must have been the last purchase this guy made. I called the credit card company and they took it off the bill."

"So, the guy sent you a *thank-you gift*?!"

"Yeah, pretty monogamous of him, huh?"

"Magnanimous."

"Whatever."

"But it wasn't, really. He paid for it with *your* credit card."

"Well, yeah…"

"So, you've been smoking these stolen cigars?"

"I thought I deserved it, given everything he put me through."

"But they're not really yours."

"I asked the credit card company if I should send them back. They said they're insured for this kind of thing. The cigar company actually already got paid. They said I could keep them."

"Unbelievable." I was shaking my head.

"So, how about we pack a few for the trip? We can both enjoy his gift together."

"I think it would be rude not to."

ONCE WE HAD ALL our gear together, we agreed to do a test ride with fully loaded panniers. I packed up my bags and weighed them—eighteen pounds. Adding a small top-tube bag, I had just over twenty pounds of gear.

I drove over to Marty's house and found him in his garage, eating the last of an apple fritter with the music blasting. Marty's garage is a former two-car space that he has converted into a combined bike shop and party room. A dozen bikes hang upside-down from the ceiling like sleeping bats. The floor is covered with spare tubes, tires, beer bottle caps, empty Doritos bags, and assorted mismatched bike gloves that haven't been washed since Obama's second term. Along the I-beam at the ceiling sit 60 or 70 different empty beer cans—souvenirs from past post-ride debriefing sessions. The walls are lined with shelves containing tools, helmets, bike shoes, energy bars, a case of beer, several cans of chili, and a Coleman propane stove. When Armageddon strikes, Marty will be hosting the tailgater.

When I arrived, Marty was still figuring out the best rack configuration for the back of his bike. Since his Paragon was an older bike, it didn't have an attachment point on the frame at the hub of his rear wheel (as mine did). So, he had bought a free-floating rack that clamped to his seat post. He attached his saddlebags to the rack, and I did the same with mine.

We mounted our bikes and took off from his garage.

Wanting to see what climbing felt like with the extra weight, we headed to the hilly Allegheny Cemetery. Just a few blocks from Marty's house, the cemetery is the final resting place of many Pittsburgh notables—songwriter Stephen Foster, Civil War General James Negley, American Revolutionary War veteran and whiskey tax collector John Neville, and many others. We entered the cemetery and hit the first hill.

What a difference twenty pounds makes.

I stood up out of my seat and pumped my legs. And pumped some more. It felt like I had a small child sitting behind me. I pedaled harder, my heart rate increasing.

Finally, we crested the hill and started gliding downward. The added weight caused me to accelerate through the descent like a rocket. Riding the brakes, we hit the bottom, then immediately began climbing again. We kept going—grinding up and gliding down—for twenty minutes, then stopped for a break.

"That was intense." I was breathing hard and in a full sweat.

"Yeah, Jumbo," said Marty. "That weight makes a difference. Now you know how I feel—I'm always carrying sixty pounds more than you, even without these bags!"

Marty looked at his rack. It had already started to shake loose from the seat post, causing his right pannier to rub against his rear tire. He got out a wrench and re-tightened it, but it was still jiggling.

"This could be a problem," he said.

Marty rigging his bike rack during the cemetery test ride

While Marty worked on his bike, I looked around. Next to us was a field with hundreds of identical white headstones. I walked over and read some of them—they were all from the 1800s. They marked the graves of Union soldiers—and a few Confederate prisoners—who had fought in the Civil War.

"This is some cemetery, Marty."

"Yeah, this is where Belle and I have decided we're gonna be buried. Eternal rest, right here, Jumbo."

"But hasn't your whole life already basically been eternal rest?" I joked.

Marty laughed and thought for a moment. "Well, more like *extended* rest."

He continued, "This is a great place to ride—I hardly ever see cars in here. Hardly see any people at all."

"All these dead people—lots of famous ones—and nobody comes to visit them? Sad," I said.

Marty nodded as he tugged on his rack. It was still swiveling on the post, but not quite as much as before.

"Well, when you die, there'll be at least one car in here," I said.

"Whose?" Marty asked.

"Mine. I'll come visit you. Since you'll be going first and all."*

"You would visit me? That'd be nice, Jumbo. How often?"

"Oh, every couple of weeks."

"Wow, that's a lot! I'd really appreciate that."

I thought a bit more. "Well, actually it might start out being every couple of weeks. But later on, I'm guessing it'll be less—probably only once a month or so."

"That's still pretty good."

"But then after a while, it might trail off to more like twice a year. How about... say... on your birthday and at Christmas?"

Marty paused.

"Hey, look, don't put yourself out, Jumbo. I know you're busy now that you're retired." He chuckled. "Here's an idea—how about you just *think* about me once a year, like when you're on a bike ride, or in a chair, or drinking a beer in the woods, or something like that?"

"Deal."

---

* Marty is three years older than Belle and five years older than Katie and me. One day we had a discussion about who will be the first to go. Belle reasoned Marty would naturally go first because he's the oldest.

"Yeah, so since I'll be the first to go, the only thing you kids need to worry about is keeping me alive," said Marty. "As long as I'm alive, you all are in the clear."

7

DEBRIS OR LITTER?

With one week to go, I was sitting in my family room when I received a FaceTime from Marty. I thought this was odd, as Marty had never Face-Time'd me before. In fact, I wasn't aware that he knew what FaceTime was. Thinking it might be something important, I immediately answered it.

"Yo, Marty, whassup?"

He didn't have his camera on, so I couldn't see him. But I could hear him having a muffled conversation with someone else.

"Marty, did you call me?!" I yelled into my phone.

"Oh... uh... is that you, Jumbo?"

"Yeah, did you butt dial me?"

"Well, it's possible. Actually, it's probable. I do have a big butt."

"Okay... well, everything good?"

"Yeah, all good," he said.

"Hey, since I have you, do you wanna get together to pack up our bikes one night this week before the trip?" I didn't want to leave this until the last minute in case we had any issues.

"Sure, let's do it at your house. How about I'll bring Belle, and we can all watch 'The Way' together?"

"Great idea. Katie will love it."

Marty and Belle came over on Thursday night before our Sunday departure. Once dinner was over, we sat down and watched the movie. We had all seen it about ten years before, but this time it held far more significance for all of us.

We watched intently as Tom (played by Martin Sheen) and his newfound pilgrim friends hike the same route Marty and I would be riding in just a few days. At the start of his journey, Tom is handed a stone to take with him and is told he will know what to do with it when the time comes. Hundreds of miles later, the group arrives at the Cruz de Ferro (the "Iron Cross"), where pilgrims leave their stones as a symbol of letting go of a burden they carry. It's a poignant scene in a very moving film.

"That trail looks harder than I thought," Marty said after the movie was over. "It's gonna be challenging."

It was time to get busy packing. I had retrieved two used boxes from a local bike shop, and I'd confirmed with the airline that we could check them as luggage as long as the weight didn't exceed 50 pounds.

We dismantled our bikes, took off the pedals, wrapped the tubes in foam padding, and deflated the tires (per airline requirements). I had also bought Apple AirTags so we could track our bikes in case they were lost by the airline or stolen while in Spain. We found a place on the frame to attach the tags, then lowered the bikes into the boxes.

Next went our helmets, and finally a shoebox that contained our pedals, tools, extra tubes, and other gear. We drilled a hole in our scallop shells, attached a string, wrapped them in foam padding, and carefully placed them into the shoebox.

We decided we would fill the panniers with all our clothes

and toiletries and carry them with us on the plane, using shoulder straps. That way, if the bike boxes were delayed, we could still get by for a couple of days.

Marty put his box in the back of his car. "I'll seal it up at home and we can meet at the airport. I think we're ready, Jumbo!"

"Sounds good, Marty. Remember, the limit is fifty pounds." That night, I weighed my box on a bathroom scale—49 pounds.

On Sunday morning, I loaded the box in our van, and Katie and I headed over to the airport. When we arrived, Belle and Marty were already there. We dragged our boxes to the ticket counter, handed the agent our passports, and told her we were flying to Pamplona.

"Put your boxes on the scale."

I went first. It read 49 pounds on the nose.

Marty went next. All four of us were staring at the display as it settled in on its final number—57 pounds. The agent shook her head.

"Can you let it slide?" Marty pleaded with the agent. "It's only seven pounds over."

"I'm sorry, sir, fifty pounds is the limit."

Belle, Katie, and I looked at Marty. "Didn't you weight it??" Belle asked, rolling her eyes. I could feel my stress level rising.

"No... but I don't know how it could be that much more than Jumbo's," said Marty.

"What do you have in there besides your bike and helmet—and that shoebox?" I asked.

"Well, I put one of my saddlebags in there. With my clothes in it."

"I thought we agreed we would carry those on." I was trying hard to conceal my frustration.

"Yeah, I know we said that, but I won't really need all those clothes during the trip over, so I thought this would be easier."

All of us were shaking our heads.

"No biggie," said Marty. He pulled the box off the scale, cut through the tape, and dug through its contents. Finally, he found the offending pannier and pulled it out. He closed up the box, re-taped it shut, and put it back on the scale.

Forty-eight pounds.

At Pittsburgh Airport. One of these things is overweight.
Which is it?

With one bag slung over each shoulder, we walked to the security checkpoint along with Katie and Belle. It was time to say goodbye. We wouldn't see them for two weeks, the longest Katie and I had ever been apart. I kissed her and gave Belle a hug.

"Jimmy, the trip is in charge now," said Belle. "Let it all happen and enjoy the ride." She knew how hard I'd worked on preparing for the journey, and how much I like things to go according to "plan."

"Yup, thanks Belle. We will!"

"Oh, and I have something to give you guys," she said, opening her purse.

Like Marty, Belle is an artist. She handed each of us a tiny handmade cloth bag. Inside each bag was a small stone.

"These are from Utah. I picked them up last summer when we were there. Carry them with you and leave them at the Iron Cross."

We thanked Belle and put the stones in our pockets. After passing through the metal detectors, we walked over to the platform to catch the tram to the airside terminal.

Our bikes were checked, and our flight was on time. We were on our way. After a stressful and busy morning, I began to relax and feel a sense of calm. I started thinking about Spain and the trip ahead.

Suddenly, I was shaken out of my tranquil state. Out of the corner of my eye, I saw what looked like red confetti spewing from Marty's body. I watched in shock as dozens of tiny red bits fell all over the platform, forming a semi-circle with a five-foot radius in front of him. My mind tried to process what was happening.

"What the...??"

"Damn! Twizzler bites!" exclaimed Marty, looking down at his feet.

"Twizzlers??" We were drawing some stares.

"Yeah, I had a whole bag of them in the front pocket of my hoodie. I tried to pull it out to eat one, and the bag broke open. Ahhhh..."

The tram was arriving. "We gotta pick these things up, Marty!" I leaned over and started gathering the pieces that had landed near me. I saw a young girl with her mother, pointing at the massive red mess and the two puerile adults who had just caused it.

Marty wasn't moving.

"Why do we need to pick them up?" he said.

"It's litter!" I said, now on my hands and knees, with two handfuls of dirty red candy in my fists. I looked around for a trash can.

"It's not litter, Jumbo, it's *debris*."

"What?!"

"It's debris. There's debris everywhere in the world. You know... dust, crumbs, loose rocks, bits of rubber from tires, stuff like that. It's all *debris*. You just leave it there."

"Come on, Marty!" I pleaded with him. "The tram!"

"Look at this plastic bag here," he said, calmly holding out the ripped—and now empty—Twizzler bag. "Now *this bag* is litter. It belongs in the trash. The candy, that's *debris*. Leave it, Jumbo."*

The tram doors opened. I tossed the candy I'd picked up into a trash can, and the two of us boarded the tram. As the doors closed, I looked through the glass at the rest of the "debris" on the floor, and at the other passengers pointing and stepping around it.

I sighed and recalled Belle's words: "The trip is in charge." Only ten minutes into our voyage, I was already questioning the trip's leadership abilities.

---

*   From the Oxford Dictionary:

Debris, *noun*: scattered pieces of waste or remains.

Litter, *noun*: trash, such as paper, cans, and bottles, that is left lying in an open or public place.

You be the judge.

8

FALSE START

Marty and I got off the tram and headed to our gate. Our journey required three flights—first to Charlotte, NC, then to Madrid, and finally to Pamplona. We had a tight connection in Charlotte, and our flight out of Pittsburgh was running late. During the flight, while Marty was relaxing with his AirPods, I was constantly checking the time. As we began our final approach into Charlotte, I estimated that we would have just fifteen minutes between landing and takeoff for the Madrid flight.

"Marty, we're landing at Gate A35. Our next flight is at Gate B5. It's probably a hundred yards. Let's both run to the gate, and whoever gets there first, ask them to hold the flight."

Marty nodded.

The plane landed. We grabbed our packs, strapped them onto our shoulders, and worked our way toward the front of the plane. At the end of the jetway, I took off.

Charlotte Airport was mobbed on this Sunday afternoon, but I had connected through here many times and knew how far I had to run. I bobbed and weaved my way through the crowd, my panniers slamming into my rib cage with every stride. I tried not to hit anyone as I dove through openings in traffic, sprinting toward the gate.

Finally, out of breath and sweating, I arrived at the gate. There were dozens of people standing around. I looked up at the board—"DELAYED." *Whew, we had time.* A few minutes later, I saw Marty sauntering down the concourse toward me. I waved to him.

"Delayed! We're okay!" I yelled. "No need to rush!" As if.

As he approached me at the gate, I told him it looked like we had another hour. We found some seats.

"Jumbo, I was watching you from behind as you took off running. Impressive! You looked like a running back weaving through that traffic. And with those saddlebags—hilarious!"

I was glad I was able to provide some entertainment for Marty in my panicked state.

Just then, I received a notification on my phone from the airline.

"CANCELLED."

It couldn't be right. I looked at the board. Indeed, they had cancelled our flight to Madrid. I broke the news to Marty.

"How can they just cancel our flight?" he asked.

"Airlines do that all the time these days." I went up to the counter and learned that it was a crew issue. We were re-scheduled for the same flight the next day.

Fortunately, I'd planned for two nights in Pamplona in case something like this happened. With the delay, we wouldn't have much time to see the city, but at least the remainder of our hotel and Airbnb reservations—in eleven different locations—would remain intact.

Disappointed and frustrated, we took the airport shuttle to the hotel provided by the airline—a Holiday Inn Express. Next to the check-in counter was a sign that advertised just what we needed:

Meditation Class
6 p.m.—9 p.m.
3rd Door on Left

Seeking serenity at the Holiday Inn Express in Charlotte

We considered joining the class mid-stream, but we were starving. After the clerk gave us our keys, we asked if she knew any places within walking distance where we could have dinner. She said that, unfortunately, nothing was that close. As we began browsing the snack offerings in the gift shop, we heard a voice from behind us.

"Pedro's. It's the best Mexican food in the area. I'll take you there."

We turned around. It was our airport shuttle driver, Ralph. He was still in the lobby and had overheard our conversation at the front desk.

"Sounds good," Marty said. "Can you give us a few minutes to put our stuff in our room?"

"Sure, I'll be here."

We dropped our bags in our room and went back downstairs. Ralph escorted us out the door, and we boarded the shuttle bus.

After driving about 200 yards, we arrived at a dilapidated concrete-and-stucco structure with large, square openings in the walls along its perimeter. In a typical building, these would be glass windows. But Pedro's seemed to go for the authentic "south of the border" open-air feel. We gave Ralph a few dollars as he dropped us off.

"Here's my cell," said Ralph. "Call me when you're ready to come back, if I don't see you before then."

See us before then? I wondered why that might be. I soon forgot about it.

We'd hoped to be on our way to Spain, about to have some local tapas. But we were in North Carolina, about to have Mexican food. Our waitress wore a name tag—"Consuela." Now it was time to try out our limited Spanish.

"*Buenas tardes, señorita,*" I said proudly.

"Buenas tardes," she responded, without breaking a smile.

"*Cerveza,*" said Marty, ordering a beer. He had learned one word in Spanish prior to our trip, and he deftly deployed it now.

"Margarita for me. And I know he'll want one too, after he finishes that beer. How about a pitcher?" I asked.

Open-air Mexican dinner near Charlotte Airport

She brought us menus along with our drinks, and we both ordered fajitas. While we waited for our food, we looked out the "window" alongside our table. With no glass or screen in the way, we had an unobstructed view of the planes flying overhead, the crumbling parking lot covered with cigarette butts, and the billboard which read "Stop Human Trafficking." I really wished someone was trafficking these two humans to Spain right now.

Our food arrived quickly. As we ate, my earlier question regarding Ralph's statement was answered. Our shuttle driver was back, this time with two couples whom we'd seen in the Holiday Inn lobby, delivering them to Pedro's. They tipped him and stepped into the restaurant.

Then, ten minutes later, Ralph reappeared with another couple. Another tip for Ralph, and two more customers for Pedro's.

"Jumbo, everyone in here is from our hotel," whispered Marty. "Ralph obviously has some kind of racket with Pedro's. He's getting it coming and going."

"Yeah, and remember how the lady at the front desk said there was nothing in walking distance? We could have easily walked here. She's probably in on it, too."

We finished our dinners, paid our waitress, and extended a "gracias." Just as I was getting ready to call Ralph, he returned with four more passengers, dropping them off for dinner. We jumped into the shuttle and rode back to the hotel. Time to get some sleep and make another try for Spain tomorrow.

9

LIFTOFF
CHARLOTTE TO MADRID

W e awoke in Charlotte to the roar of planes overhead. This was the first time we'd unpacked and re-packed our panniers, something we would do many times as the trip went along. We were in no hurry, as our plane wasn't leaving until 4:00 p.m. We checked out and boarded the shuttle, now driven by a woman named Rebecca.

"Any luck this morning?" I asked Marty.

"You kidding? One day in? Not a chance. Just hoping it happens soon after we get to Spain."

Besides his poor eyesight, Marty's other physical frailty is that he has difficulty staying regular outside of a 30-mile radius of his home. It's an extreme form of a condition experienced by many people when they travel, yet it is very specific in terms of the distance. It's precisely 30 miles. No more, no less.

"Sorry, man," I offered in sympathy.

"How are you feeling today, Jumbo?"

"Actually, I'm feeling pretty good. Top of my game today. After all, I stayed at a Holiday Inn Express last night!"

Back in the Charlotte Airport, we made our way to the airline club lounge to wait for our flight. During my days in corporate America, I would visit this same lounge several times a month while waiting for connecting flights. I looked over at the carrells where the "old me" would sit—laptop open, headset on, scrambling to get work done or finish a conference call before my next flight. This was a Monday, and the carrells were full of people doing just that.

"Jumbo, look at all of them. They're less than two feet apart, their faces buried in their computers. They have no idea who the person next to them even is. You actually *did that*?"

"I sure did. Well, not my *entire* career. Only for the last... oh, thirty years or so. We didn't have laptops until the early '90s."

"It's amazing you can still function as a human being."

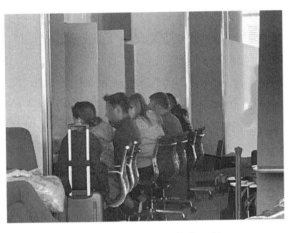

Reminders of the "Old Me" at Charlotte Airport

Finally, it was time to board the plane. Once we settled into our seats, Marty looked as if he needed something to do.

"Here, Marty, I've got something you're gonna like." I reached into my bag, pulled out a laminated sheet, and handed it to him.

"Whoa, Jumbo, what's this?"

"It's our full itinerary. One row for each day, color-coded. Where we're going, what we'll see, where we're staying, mileage, elevation, etc. I laminated it so we can use it the whole trip, even in the rain. I made two—one for each of us."

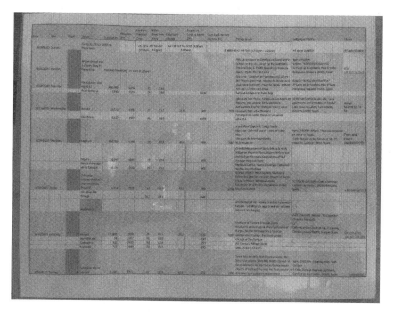

Laminated itinerary

"Jumbo, this is some serious 'seeing what you can do.' Looks like a football play sheet." Marty held the sheet up to his face, covering his mouth as if he were a coach disguising his lip movements. "Flea flicker... Jumbo, go long down the sideline..."

"Nice work," he said as he began studying the sheet.

It was a seven-hour overnight flight, and we attempted to get some sleep in our cramped coach seats. I was awake nearly the entire night and got up twice to use the bathroom. Marty never left his seat.

We landed in Madrid around 8:00 a.m. local time and started making our way off the plane.

"Pinch yourself, Jumbo, we're in Spain!" said Marty.

"Did you get any sleep?" I asked.

"A little, not much."

"Me neither," I said. "Did you even use the bathroom? I didn't see you get up."

"Jumbo, in my entire sixty-five years, I have never used an airplane bathroom. Not once."

"What? Seriously? Why not?" We were heading down the jetway into the terminal.

"They're gross."

"How do you know if you've never been in one?"

"Well, I guess I don't actually know. But I've been in the back row next to the bathroom enough times to know what they smell like."

"They're not that bad inside, Marty."

"Well, at this point, I have a perfect streak. Sixty-five years, Jumbo. It's like Cal Ripken's Iron Man streak—it's at that level."

Marty was referring to the 2,632 consecutive games played by the Baltimore Orioles' shortstop over sixteen years, sometimes while injured or sick. I'm sure Cal would have been flattered by the comparison.

"Ripken? Your streak is that level, huh?" I joked.

"Yes it is, and I'm not about to break it."

10

NO BIKE DAY
MADRID TO PAMPLONA

We waited at the gate in Madrid for our final leg to Pamplona. At one point, it occurred to me to check on the status of our bikes, given our flight was a day late. I opened up the "Find My" app on my phone and was relieved to see the AirTags report that they were indeed at Madrid Airport. We were exhausted, but we were getting closer, and our bikes had made it across the ocean.

To double check, I went up to the counter and asked whether we needed to do anything special to make sure our boxes made it onto the last flight.

"You don't need to do anything," said the gate agent. "Your bikes are checked as luggage. Your luggage always follows you."

Satisfied, we boarded the plane. The Pamplona flight would take less than an hour, and I tried desperately to get some shut-eye. Alas, sleep would not come, and I sat there, wide awake. I recalled I would often have the same challenge on my many business trips to Europe as the "old me." I just needed to get through this day—I knew I'd sleep well tonight.

Restless, I broke out my guidebook and began reading about Pamplona.

Over the next eleven days, Marty and I would travel through three regions of Spain—Navarre, León, and Galicia. Pamplona is the capital city of the Navarre region—it sits at an elevation of nearly 1,500 feet in the foothills of the Pyrenees, a mountain range that runs along the border between Spain and France, peaking at just over 11,000 feet. With a population of around 200,000, it's the largest city we would visit on this trip.

Made famous by its annual "Running of the Bulls," Pamplona has a long and storied history. It's in the heart of Basque Country—the Basque people inhabited much of south-western Europe (including the Pyrenees) for centuries before invaders from other areas of Europe and the Middle East came to call.

First were the Romans, led by General Pompey in 75 BC. He established a camp here and, like any good Roman general, named the city after himself, calling it "Pompaelo." Their reign lasted about 500 years, until the Visigoths, a Germanic group living in Southern Gaul (now France), came over the Pyrenees, conquered Pamplona, and ruled the area for the next 300 years.

In the 700s, Pamplona (and, in fact, most of Spain) was the target of two invasions by Muslim groups—the Umayyads and the Moors—coming from northern Africa across the Strait of Gibraltar. The Christians battled the Moors throughout the country for the next 700 years in what became known as the Reconquest.

Marty and I knew almost nothing about Spanish history prior to our trip. But we did know about the Moors. How? From watching the comedy show "Seinfeld," our go-to source of educational content.*

---

* In the Seinfeld episode about the "Bubble Boy," George is playing Trivial Pursuit with a boy who lives in a germ-free plastic bubble. The boy continually taunts George, and after a while, George has had enough. When George reads the question: "Who invaded Spain in the eighth century?" the boy correctly answers "The Moors." But because of a misprint, the card says "Moops." George

"Marty," I said. "It says here the Moors invaded Spain in the eighth century."

He was trying to sleep. "Don't you mean 'Moops?'"

"Moors!" I corrected him with a smile.

"Moops!" Marty exclaimed.

We both giggled, and I continued reading.

After the Reconquest, Spanish rule in Pamplona lasted for several centuries until the Napoleonic Wars in the early 1800s. In 1808, French troops came over the Pyrenees using the same route that had been used for centuries by Camino pilgrims, now called the "Napoleon Pass." Napoleon's troops seized Pamplona and occupied it until 1813, when France was forced to surrender following a blockade by the Spanish army.

Because of all this activity, Pamplona has a rich mix of history and architecture. After reading about it, I lamented that we would have very little time to see the city. We would need to make the most of the time we had.

As the plane made its approach to Pamplona, I looked out the window at the Pyrenees. Somewhere out there was the Napoleon Pass, where pilgrims were just getting started on their trek towards Santiago, probably excited but also feeling some pain. Maybe we would meet some of them in Pamplona.

We disembarked and walked to the baggage area. After all the other passengers had retrieved their bags, the conveyor stopped moving. We looked around—there was no sign of our bike boxes. In fact, no sign of anyone at all. I opened my "Find My" app and was shocked.

"Madrid!" I said, shaking my head in disbelief. "Marty, the bikes are still in Madrid!"

"What?! No way."

---

refuses to give him credit, and they scream back and forth at each other "Moors!" "Moops!" A battle ensues, the boy's bubble is punctured and deflates, and well... you get the picture.

"Yup, look." I showed him my phone screen.

We had been awake for over 30 hours, and any benefit I'd received from sleeping at the Holiday Inn Express had long since faded away. I was having a hard time containing my frustration.

We walked around and finally found a woman who looked like she worked there.

"*Habla Inglés?*" I tested out one of the five or six Spanish phrases I'd learned.

"A little," she replied in English.

"Our bikes didn't make it on the flight. They are still in Madrid."

"How do you know?" she asked.

I showed her my phone and gave her our baggage claim tags.

"Let me see." She stepped behind the desk and tapped on her computer.

"You are right! They are indeed in Madrid!" she declared with a smile, seeming oddly excited that our bikes were 250 miles away. I was not excited.

"Here, you need to fill out this lost baggage claim form. To check on the status, you can call this number and give them the tracking number. They can give you updates."

We filled out the form, handed it to her, and took a copy for ourselves.

"When will they get here? Can we get them tonight?" I implored.

"There is one more flight from Madrid to Pamplona tonight. If there is room, they can take the boxes on that plane."

"What if there isn't room? You're saying there is a chance it may not happen?!" I was losing it.

"Yes, and if not, they will try again tomorrow." The woman then turned and walked away.

Try again? Tomorrow? We needed to start riding the

following morning in order to make it to the next town—Estella—by Wednesday night. Otherwise, I would need to change the remaining eleven hotel and Airbnb reservations, as well as our flight home. I was deliriously tired and could feel my blood pressure increasing. I stomped my feet and slammed my fist on the counter.

The trip is in charge.

Pamplona Airport, without bikes.

11

THE RUNNING OF THE MARTY
PAMPLONA

Exhausted and angry, we stepped out of the airport and looked for a taxi. Fortunately, we had to wait about a half-hour, which gave me time to cool down. Eventually, a taxi arrived, and I gave the driver the address to our Airbnb.

After a short ride, we pulled up in front of the building. Our host, Guillermo, came out and met us. He showed us around the apartment and, in perfect English, gave us some recommendations on where to eat. We told him about our bikes.

"*Bicigrinos?*" he asked.

"Excuse me?" I replied.

"Bicigrinos. It's Spanish for 'biking pilgrims.' Those on foot are called *peregrinos.*"

"That's us—bicigrinos. But until we find our bikes, I guess we're actually peregrinos too," I said dejectedly.

Guillermo offered to help locate our bikes, and we gave him our tracking number. We then said goodbye and thanked him for all his assistance.

The apartment was delightful. It was a two-bedroom flat on the fourth floor of a building on Estafeta Street, one of the three streets used for the "Running of the Bulls." The living room opened to a balcony with a view of the town, of Estafeta Street below, and of the Pyrenees in the distance.

Marty and I headed out and began a sleep-starved walking tour of Pamplona.

In medieval times, this was a walled city, and sections of the stone ramparts are still well-preserved. We walked along them, then stepped under the Portal de Francia, the gate through which travelers from France would enter the city. Camino pilgrims coming off the Napoleon Pass have traversed this opening since it was built in the 1500s; Napoleon's troops also used it in the early 1800s. Marty and I spotted two women with large backpacks, moving slowly and limping, as they exchanged a "high five" and took a selfie under the archway.

Portal de Francia, Pamplona

We made a short loop, taking in the Baroque Ayuntamiento (City Hall) building, the Iglesia (church) de San Saturnino, and the highlight—the 15th century Gothic Pamplona Cathedral, built on the site of the original Roman village of Pompaelo. We toured the interior of the cathedral, the first of many we would see over the next two weeks.

"Marty, any idea what makes something 'Gothic?'" Marty had studied architecture in art school, and I suspected he would know the answer.

"See those big stained glass windows? And how open it is in here? That's Gothic," said Marty. "Gothic came after the Romanesque period. Romanesque architecture has thick walls and small windows. The walls had to provide the support since they hadn't yet invented those flying buttresses to brace the walls from the outside."

"What about Baroque?"

"That came after the Gothic period. Baroque architecture is more ornate and elaborate, like the City Hall we just saw."

How was Marty able to sound so coherent on such little sleep? My brain felt like scrambled eggs.

Pamplona Cathedral

At the cathedral, we bought what would become a well-used travel companion during our entire journey—our Pilgrim Passports. We would need to get these stamped at least twice per day to qualify for our Compostela certificates at the end of

our ride in Santiago. The attendant at the church gave us our
first stamps.

Pilgrim Passports

While sitting on a bench in front of the cathedral, I tried
calling the baggage phone number to check on the status of our
bikes, but the language barrier was too challenging. I eventually gave up.

Just then, my phone rang. It was Guillermo.

"Did you hear anything about the bikes?" he asked.

"No, and I can't seem to communicate with the baggage
department at the airline. They only speak Spanish."

"I will call them for you. Maybe I'll have better luck. I'll give
you an update after I speak with them."

I couldn't believe he would do this for us. "Thank you so
much, Guillermo."

By this time, it was late, and we were hungry. Pamplona is
known for *pinxtos*, the Basque version of tapas. We found an
outdoor café on the Plaza de Castile and sampled some of the
local fare. I added an order of *patatas bravas* (spicy potatoes),
something we would see on menus everywhere throughout
Spain. We were amazed at how inexpensive the food was.

Pinxtos in Pamplona, Plaza de Castile

While we were eating dinner, Guillermo called again.

"I tried calling the baggage department, but they couldn't give me the information," he said. "So, I drove to the airport and talked to an agent there. She said your bikes made it on the last plane from Madrid, so I waited and saw them come out in the baggage area. They wouldn't let me pick them up for you, but they are delivering them to your Airbnb right now. You should get back there quickly."

"You went all the way to the airport for us? Wow. We can't thank you enough," I said. He was like an angel.

"They'll be delivering them in a white van," said Guillermo. "But cars aren't allowed on Estafeta Street at this time of day, so you'll need to meet them at the top of the street and drag the boxes to the apartment."

We paid our bill and walked quickly toward our building. We weren't sure which end was the "top" of Estafeta Street, so Marty walked to one end and I walked to the other, about 100 yards apart, both looking for a white van. Marty spotted the vehicle, stopped the driver, and unloaded the boxes. He texted and said he was heading toward me.

Now, allow me to change the point of view for a moment. I'm sorry to ask you to move, but I'm going to place you in a seat in an outdoor café on Estafeta Street. You are a native Pamplonian, enjoying some pinxtos and a glass of Rioja on a warm evening with your partner. You've experienced Pamplona's "Running of the Bulls" in July many times, and have even participated in the wild animal chase along this very street on several of those occasions. But this is September, and the town and this street are quiet and peaceful.

Suddenly, as you take a sip of your wine, you see two graying men at opposite ends of the street, wearing matching shirts that say "Get Up and Ride." One of them, slight of stature with bags under his eyes, is waving wildly and screaming "Marty! Marty!" The other one, large and burly, is dragging two huge cardboard bike boxes down the street toward the smaller man—grunting heavily and yelling "Got 'em, Jumbo! Got 'em!"

You've seen just about everything in this town, and very little phases you. But you've seen nothing like this before. You roll your eyes and whisper to your partner *"Americanos locos"* (crazy Americans).

Yes, it was "The Running of the Marty," Pamplona's first bike-box-pulling event, and Marty was doing admirably well for his maiden outing.

I walked briskly toward him, taking in the amused expressions of people having dinner at cafés as he muscled the boxes over the cobblestones.

The "Running of the Marty," Estafeta Street, Pamplona

We met at the center of the street, near the entrance to our apartment. With some effort, we got the boxes onto the elevator and into the apartment. As exhausted as we were at this point, we knew we still had work to do.

We unpacked the boxes and began assembling our bikes. After an hour, we had them together and ready to go for the following morning. As a finishing touch, we tied our scallop shells onto the outside of our panniers.

"Excuse me for a bit, Jumbo." Marty headed to the bathroom.

Fighting to stay awake until it got dark, I stepped onto the balcony with my guidebook to read more about Spain and Pamplona.

As I was reading, the term "Middle Ages" kept coming up. While "middle age" could certainly describe Marty and me (generously, I might add, given we are in our sixties), when capitalized, the "Middle Ages" refers to the nearly 1000-year time period in Europe between the end of Roman civilization (fifth century) and the Renaissance (14th to 16th centuries). The Middle Ages are best known for things you see in "Game of

Thrones" and "Monty Python"—castles, knights, armored horses, and gory punishments.

The "Middle Ages" is synonymous with the "Medieval Era." It's also sometimes called the "Dark Ages" because of the lack of scientific and cultural advancement during this time. By 450 AD, it seems everyone assumed the Romans had already invented everything. So they "chilled" for roughly ten centuries until guys like DaVinci and Michelangelo came along and started working on some new stuff.

Think about that for a minute. An entire millennium went by, and the best historians can come up with is to say that it was in the "middle." A write-off. A pass-through. At least calling it "dark" is saying it was *something*. Yet the "Renaissance," which lasted a mere 200 years, is a name now proudly affixed to fancy clothing lines, fragrances, festivals, a high-end hotel chain, and certain cultured men who possess a wider range of talents beyond simply watching football and using power tools. It doesn't seem fair.

In the "Middle Ages," much of Europe was under a feudal system. Spain was made up of many kingdoms—León, Aragon, Asturias, Galicia, Navarre, Castile, and several others.

The Crown of Castile was the most dominant kingdom, and it became a powerful global empire in the 16th century (think King Ferdinand and Queen Isabella). Castile was the kingdom behind Christopher Columbus' expedition, the discovery of the Pacific Ocean, the conquests of the Aztec and Incan empires, and the demise of many Moors. Castile was also busy annexing other kingdoms in Spain into its empire, and in 1512, Castile annexed Navarre and made Pamplona the capital of the region.

AFTER ABOUT HALF AN HOUR, Marty reappeared.

"Got a bit of an issue here, Jumbo."

"What?" I set down my book.

"Did you have any reaction to that Mexican food in Charlotte?"

"No, I'm good. No problems."

"Well, I think it's hitting me hard. Hopefully I'll be okay by tomorrow."

"Damn, that sucks, Marty." I thought for a moment. "But hey, look on the bright side, you're well outside your thirty-mile radius, and you've already taken care of business!"

"That didn't count," declared Marty, shaking his head and wagging his finger.

"What?"

"Didn't count. That was tainted food. I'm not counting it."

"But it still happened, right? There's no denying it. It definitely counts."

"Nope. Doesn't count."

"Counts."

Marty paused. "Well, at best there's an asterisk, Jumbo."

"Okay, an asterisk. And here's some Imodium. It should help."

I handed him the pills. He hesitated for a moment, knowing they could certainly help his immediate situation, but might also cost him longer-term. He shrugged, popped one in his mouth, and washed it down with water.

We collapsed into our beds. My body finally gave in, and sleep came within seconds.

12

ENCIERRO

PAMPLONA

After a long, deep slumber, I was gently awakened by the sun peeking through my window. I made coffee and stepped onto the balcony. The sky was clear and blue, and the sun was rising over the Pyrenees. Four stories below, the street cleaners had just come through, and the cobblestones were wet and glistening in the emerging light. A delivery truck was unloading supplies into one of the cafés. I detected a faint whiff of croissants.

Having slept well, I felt like a completely different human being. Marty joined me on the balcony a few minutes later.

"Coffee's ready, Marty. How ya feeling?"

"Much better, Jumbo. I think I'll be fine today. Wow—what a beautiful day. Look at that sky!"

"We're riding only thirty miles today to Estella. Should take around three hours. So we have some time this morning. Want to check out more of Pamplona before we head out?"

"Sure, let's do it."

We left the apartment with our empty bike cartons, looking for a dumpster. We found a recycle bin just down the street, broke down the boxes, and stuffed the cardboard inside. Next we strolled over to Pamplona's most famous landmark—the Plaza de Toros—the bullring.

The Festival of San Fermin (Navarre's patron saint) is Pamplona's biggest event of the year, occurring over nine days each July. Its centerpiece is the "Running of Bulls." These "bull runs," or *encierros*, occur in cities all over Spain, usually as part of a summertime festival. They involve running in front of six to ten bulls that have been let loose in the streets.

Originally, encierros had a practical aspect. They were used to move bulls from fields outside the city to the bullring, where they would be killed by matadors in the evening's bullfight. Today, they are mainly events where daring, inebriated men risk their lives while spectators watch from the balconies above.

Pamplona's encierro is the largest in Spain, and a bull run occurs on eight of the nine days of the festival. Pamplona sets up wooden fences to direct the bulls along the route and block off side streets, with small gaps to allow runners to escape if things get dicey. The total time for each event is only two to three minutes, with a distance of about half a mile.

Every year, between 50 and 100 people are injured during the run. Most are from intoxication or people getting jammed up at the "exits." However, people do occasionally get gored—in 2013, six runners ended up on the business end of the horns. Since record-keeping began in 1910, sixteen people have died.

Marty and I circled the bullring. Above the main entrance was hung a 50-foot banner with an artist's rendering of a matador with the head of a bull. Another banner depicted a matador dressed in a Superman costume. And across the street, the Monument de Encierro captured the chaos of the entire scene in bronze—complete with men being trampled by bulls on a mission.

"You think you'd ever want to do that, Jumbo?"

"I was once chased by a German Shepherd for two blocks as a kid. I think I'll pass."

Plaza de Toros (The Bullring)

Monument de Encierro

We walked back to the cathedral, where we'd learned that a tour is given of the bell tower at 11:30 a.m. each day. Arriving just in time, we ascended the stone stairway to the top. In addition to seeing the bells up close, we were rewarded with a stunning view of the entire city of Pamplona and the Pyrenees beyond. Small patches of white clouds moved slowly overhead and stretched all the way to the horizon. We gazed at the hills to the southwest—we would be biking there in less than an hour.

Bell Tower, Pamplona Cathedral

We made our way back down the narrow stairs and took one more look inside the spectacular cathedral. In front of the altar, a renewal of vows was taking place by a Spanish couple in their eighties. I was in a better frame of mind than the day before, and I knelt in one of the side chapels. I thanked God for this gift of the Camino trip and asked for him to watch over Marty and me on our journey.

Octogenarian renewal of vows at Pamplona Cathedral

ALTO DEL PERDÓN

THE HILL OF FORGIVENESS - PAMPLONA TO ESTELLA

I t was time to ride.

We headed back to our apartment, packed up our panniers, and took our bikes down in the elevator. Opening the front door, we emerged onto Estafeta Street, now a lively lunchtime scene with people strolling, dining, and shopping. At our feet, we spotted the first of hundreds of Camino markers we would see during our journey—a metal scallop shell with a bicycle icon, set among the cobblestones. It was a beautiful sunny day; we mounted our bikes and were on our way.

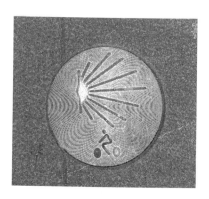

"Pinch yourself, Jumbo!" said Marty. "We're riding our bikes in Spain!"

We rode the sidewalks and streets toward the southwestern edge of the city, passing through La Ciudadela (the Citadel), a former Renaissance military fort built in the 16th century.

Soon we arrived at the small village of Cizur Menor, the last suburb on this side of Pamplona and the last sign of civilization we would have for a while. Looking to the west, we saw what would become a familiar vista—vast, open fields, hay bales, an occasional patch of trees, and a medieval building here and there. Snaking through this landscape was a unidirectional gravel path—the Camino de Santiago.

Starting on the Camino outside of Pamplona

As our tires left the road and started on the track, we were immediately glad we'd brought heavy duty mountain bikes. The Camino is really made for walking, and the surface on this section was rough. We felt the jostling of our saddlebags on the backs of our bikes as we rode up a gradual incline.

Just outside of Cizur Menor, we passed a group of Camino pilgrims. They were wearing large backpacks and were using trekking poles to pick their way along the trail. Attached to the back of each of their packs was a white scallop shell.

"*Buen Camino!*" they said as we passed by.

"Buen Camino!" we repeated. This was the first of many such exchanges we would make over the coming days.

As we rode along, the hill got steeper, and a small stream appeared alongside the trail. At one point, it actually flowed across the Camino. Our wheels easily rolled through it, kicking up a small spray. We passed more pilgrims, all heading in the same direction.

We worked our way up the incline, walking our bikes periodically as the surface became rockier.

About halfway up, we met two mountain bikers heading down the hill toward us. They didn't have packs of any kind—they were out for a day ride. And they were bleeding.

We stopped and dismounted.

"What happened?" I asked.

"Rocks... fell... scrape..." They were Spanish and did their best to relay in English the danger of what lay ahead.

One had skinned his arm from his elbow to his wrist; the other was bleeding from his knee.

"You okay?" Marty asked.

"Sí, okay." They didn't seem too bothered by their wounds. "Watch out."

"Adios, gracias," I said.

"Buen Camino," they said as they passed us down the hill.

"Be careful up ahead, Jumbo," said Marty. "Those guys look

like experienced bikers. If they took a spill, we gotta watch it, especially with all this extra weight."

The ascent we were tackling was the Alto del Perdón, the "Hill of Forgiveness." It's named for a 13th century basilica dedicated to Nuestra Señora del Perdón (Our Lady of Atonement), which was destroyed by Napoleon's troops. Even without the church, it's aptly named—we were paying some serious penance as we struggled uphill.

Finally, we arrived at the top, where we were rewarded with a sweeping 360-degree view of the entire valley, including the outskirts of Pamplona to the northeast. At the summit sits an iconic Camino metal sculpture of pilgrims and donkeys. Etched on one figure is a phrase which aptly captures the scene:

DONDE SE CRUZA EL CAMINO DEL VIENTO

CON EL DE LAS ESTRELLAS

(WHERE THE PATH OF WIND CROSSES WITH THE STARS)

Alto del Perdón, The Hill of Forgiveness

We took in the view and snapped a few pictures. A man on a road bike with skinny tires, loaded with heavy saddlebags, approached us and asked if we would take his picture. He was from France and spoke almost no English. After taking the shot with his phone, I tried using my limited high school French to communicate.

"*Tu... seul?*" I wanted to know if he was riding solo.

"*Oui. C'est très difficile!*" He confirmed he was alone, and said it was "very difficult."

"*Oui,*" I replied. "*Je m'appelle Jim. Uh... Il est... Marty,*" I said, introducing ourselves.

"*Enchanté. Patrice,*" he said, extending his hand.

Using hand signals and bits of French, we learned that Patrice had begun his journey from his home in Northern France and had ridden the length of the country to St. Jean Pied de Port. He had then walked his bike over the Napoleon Pass, and had also pushed it most of that morning up the Alto del Perdón. We couldn't understand why anyone would attempt this ride on a lightweight road bike, without the benefit of the wide tires and shock absorbers Marty and I had on our mountain bikes.

Patrice

Looking around the hilltop, we saw a school bus parked across from the metal sculpture. Inside, coffee was being served to pilgrims who wanted to get out of the sun. Many other pilgrims were taking a break at the summit, and nearly all of them had their shoes off.

By this point, the walkers who had started in France were about four or five days into their trek, and many were already nursing blisters. We met Maria, from the Netherlands, who had hiked from Bordeaux to St. Jean and then over the Pyrenees. She chatted with us while rubbing her feet, her smile unable to disguise the pain she was clearly feeling.

After a short break, we began heading down the Hill of Forgiveness. The descent made the trip up seem like a leisurely cruise on the GAP Trail. Here, the path consisted of a deep layer of large, loose rocks. It was like trying to ride on a dry creek bed —downhill. My rear tire slipped several times, causing my feet to un-clip from the pedals. I caught myself before I went down.

The rough riding was also taking a toll on Marty's rear rack, which was suffering under the weight of his panniers. As in the cemetery during our training ride, his rack was twisting on his seat post, causing one of his bags to rub against his rear wheel. In fact, one of the support bars on the rack itself had already broken. He stopped to wrap the remaining bars together using duct tape and zip ties.

"You know what this is called, Jumbo?"

"What?"

"Rigging."

With over 400 miles to go, we both sensed trouble ahead.

After attempting to ride the rocky slope for a few more minutes, we concluded it was impossible and got off our bikes. We walked them down the path past a group of pilgrims, one of whom had just twisted her ankle. Patrice was just behind us, also walking his bike.

Halfway down the hill, we spotted a paved two-lane road which went off to the side. It appeared to run parallel to the

Camino and had a fairly wide shoulder. Marty and I decided it was time for a new game plan.

"How far have we gone?" Marty asked.

"About nine or ten miles. In two hours." Our pace was less than five miles an hour. At this rate, it would take us until Thanksgiving to get to Santiago.

Marty wiped his face with his bandana. "Do you think this road would get us there, Jumbo? I gotta give my rack a break from these rocks."

"Gimme a minute—I'll look it up."

I got out my phone and opened Google Maps. We had purchased a travel wi-fi device in the Madrid Airport, which was about the size of a deck of cards and acted as a mobile hotspot. This gave us high-speed internet access pretty much anywhere in Spain without having to rely on our cell phone service. Hotspots, AirTags, smartphones, GPS... medieval pilgrims were downright prehistoric compared to Marty and me in 2023.

I pulled out my laminated sheet and saw that the next major town on the way to Estella was Puente la Reina. I entered it into Google Maps and found a route which would use the road we'd just discovered.

"Let's try the road," I said to Marty.

I looked up from my phone and realized Patrice was standing there, looking at us.

"Uh... the... road... *la... route,*" I said, pointing at the road and struggling to find the French words. "*Nous... take... la route.*" *How do you say "take?"* It was buried somewhere deep in the recesses of my brain, along with a thousand other things I hadn't used since tenth grade.

As I reached for my phone to bring up my Translate app, Patrice shook his head and pointed at the rocky trail below. "Camino," he said.

Why wouldn't he take the road, given it looked so much easier? Did he know something we didn't?

"Okay... uh... *d'accord. Au revoir*, Patrice!" I said, waving.

Marty and I got on the road and began our descent. As our speed picked up and cars whizzed by, I was nervous. Each time I heard a car behind me, I looked over my shoulder to see how close it was. But the drivers gave us plenty of room, and after a while I felt more at ease.

At the bottom of the hill, we passed through the small village of Uterga, and soon afterwards arrived at Puente la Reina ("Queen's Bridge"). We had ridden about fifteen miles from Pamplona at this point, and Puente la Reina is where most walkers stop for the night.

We rode along the center street, passing a number of cafés and peering down the town's quaint medieval alleys. Upon exiting the village, we pedaled over a bridge—one of many built in the Middle Ages to enable pilgrims to cross rivers on their way to Santiago de Compostela. This bridge, with six beautiful stone arches, spanned 350 feet across the River Arga and was built in the 11th century by Queen Alberta. It was named "Queen's Bridge" after the royal lady.

Puente la Reina ("Queen's Bridge")

Marty and I stopped for a quick water break and an energy bar, then continued on the road toward Estella. On this stretch, there were very few cars, and we were able to ride side-by-side. We were also making much better time compared to our slog during the first part of the day. But we did wonder if we were missing something by not being on the Camino path.

The road took us through rolling farmland and picturesque countryside. It was mid-afternoon, the sun was high in the sky, and it was a comfortable 75 degrees—perfect. We relaxed, and Marty and I chatted as we cruised along.

"Jumbo, this is something, huh? A couple of old geezers out here, riding across Spain. Not bad for a couple of old timers, huh?"

"Yup, can you believe it? In our sixties. Not bad at all."

"You know, if we keep this up we can ride in our old age, Jumbo."

"I sure hope so," I said, knowing full well that the "new me" was already in its fourth quarter.

I breathed in the sweet Spanish air. We were pedaling easily as we watched the landscape pass by.

"How many years you think you got left?" I asked Marty.

"How many years of biking, you mean?"

"No, like, how many years total?"

"Oh." Marty thought for a moment. "Fourteen and a half."

"What?"

"Fourteen and half years," Marty repeated confidently.

"Why so specific?" I looked over at him, puzzled.

"I'm shooting for eighty. Seems like a good age, huh? That's fourteen and a half years away."

"So, you're just gonna go out on your eightieth birthday? With a bang?"

"Yeah, that's what I'm thinking. Why drag things out?" We were cackling at this point.

"How many years you think you got left, Jumbo?"

"Well, I don't really know, hopefully at least thirty."

"*Thirty?* You think you've got *thirty years* left? So you're telling me there'll be a ninety-year-old Jumbo someday?"

"Well, I don't know... living to ninety *is* a stretch. Maybe twenty-five is more realistic."

"Really? *Twenty-five years?* You think you've got twenty-five years in you?"

"I dunno... maybe you're right... maybe only twenty."

Marty suddenly pulled over on the shoulder and stopped. I pulled over next to him. He looked at me with a serious expression.

"Jumbo, you know what you just did?"

"What?"

"You just gave up ten years. Just like that." He snapped his fingers. "In an instant. *Ten years.*"

"Well, maybe I spoke too soon. Actually, now that I think about it, twenty-five to thirty is more like it."

"Nope, it's too late Jumbo. You gave 'em up. Ten years. *Poof!* Gone."

"No way for me to get them back?"

"Nope."

I stood there silently.

Marty continued, "But, hey, it really doesn't matter to me since I'll be gone first. So, whether it's twenty or thirty more years for you, I won't be around to see it anyway."

I shook my head as we began moving again. While I pedaled along and reflected, I felt a little sad that I'd truncated my life in a five-minute conversation on the Camino. But I guess that's what the Camino is all about—finding yourself.

This was only the first day. I started making a list of things to tell Katie when I got home.

14

NECESITO UNA CERVEZA
ESTELLA

Two hours later, we arrived in Estella. We had ridden only 30 miles with around 2,500 feet of climbing, yet it had taken five hours, and we were wiped out. It was around 5:00 p.m.—the village was strangely quiet, with just a few people strolling along the main street and two kids kicking a soccer ball. We would come to learn that this is the "dead zone" in Spain. Virtually everything shuts down in the late afternoon.

Also known by its Basque name, Lizarra, Estella is a town of about 13,000 people at the western edge of Basque Country in Navarre. It was founded in 1090 and quickly became a stopover on the Camino. This brought in many people from around Europe, some settling here and making the town wealthy. In the late 12th century, the royal palace of the Kings and Queens of Navarre was located here, bringing even more prosperity.

If you closed your eyes and tried to imagine a classic medieval Spanish village, you'd be picturing Estella. It has all the elements—centuries-old churches, cobblestone streets, plazas graced with fountains and cafés, arched stone bridges over a slow-moving river, a castle, a palace, and Airbnb.

Marty and I passed several magnificent Romanesque build-ings as we pedaled toward our apartment. We found our room, checked in, and showered. I was pleasantly surprised and grateful to find a washing machine in the flat, knowing that pilgrims in the albergues were probably hand-washing their clothes in sinks at this moment. I threw our dirty clothes into the washer, and we headed outside to find a place for dinner.

Just around the corner was a plaza—we picked a café and sat down. Next to us was a Spanish couple drinking beer out of large mugs. The man's shirt had an image of a gas tank on empty with the words *Necesito Una Cerveza* (I need a beer). We necesito'd one too, and since he appeared to have some experi-ence with the subject, we thought we'd ask him what was in his mug so we could order the same.

Running on empty in Estella

"Ho-la, what-o kind-o cerveza... you drink-o?" Marty asked, pointing at the guy's beer.

Rather than actually learning Spanish, Marty had adopted a strategy of adding an "o" to the ends of his words in hopes the locals would understand.

The man looked at us blankly.

"*Que... cerveza... tu?*" I tried using some choppy Spanish I'd picked up from a few hours spent on Duolingo.

"*Grande,*" he answered. It was obvious to us that it was a large beer. It was also obvious we weren't going to find out what *kind* of beer he was drinking.

When the waitress arrived, I pointed at the man's beer and said, "*Dos—cervezas—grande, por favor?*"

Soon, two big frosty mugs were set in front of us.

"Day one, Jumbo, nice work." Marty held his glass up, and I clinked mine against his. We took our first sips and began recounting the day.

"I can't believe we rode only thirty miles today. It feels like sixty," said Marty.

"Yeah, the first half was brutal. But hey, only 420 miles to go!"

We talked about all that had happened—our morning in Pamplona, the Alto del Perdón, meeting Patrice, and riding on the road. We also discussed Marty's rack and its trail-worthiness for the coming days.

We were getting hungry, so I motioned to the waitress. "Menus?"

She pointed to her watch. "*Siete.*" I guess that meant they weren't serving food until 7:00 p.m. It was only ten minutes away, so we enjoyed our beers while we waited.

Soon, she brought over the menus, which were entirely in Spanish. I started using my Translate app to identify the choices.

"How about I ask Sam?" Marty took a picture and texted it to his son (in Zurich) who is fluent in Spanish. Sam immediately responded and told us what to order. We had white bean soup, prosciutto and melon, bacala (cod), lamb, and flan for dessert. Everything was delicious.

We finished our dinner, paid our bill, and asked the waitress to stamp our passports. Marty and I then walked around the town, which had come alive after dark on this Wednesday evening.

We popped into a lively bar, filled with locals who spoke virtually no English. We managed to learn that one of them—Antonio—had ridden his e-bike from Seville all the way to Santiago de Compostela the previous year. Using gestures, we told him that we were riding bikes without motors. His facial expression seemed to say "*Americanos locos.*"

We went back to our apartment and discussed the plan for the next day. With another relatively short ride—30 miles to Logroño—we decided we would tour Estella in the early morning and aim to head out by around 10:00 a.m. Day one on the Camino was in the books.

15

WATER INTO WINE
ESTELLA

Morning arrived in Estella. Marty was up before me —he had already found a nearby café where he'd enjoyed a cappuccino and a pastry. He brought me a chocolate croissant, and I made myself an espresso using the machine in our room. I could tell he was excited.

"Jumbo, it's another beautiful day out there. And the street markets are just getting set up. Gonna be a great day for a ride!"

The caffeine and sugar gave me the jolt I needed to get started. My back was sore from the rough ride the previous day, so I emptied an ice tray from the freezer into a plastic bag and pressed it into my lumbar area. Then I tossed down a couple of Advil tablets. Soon the pain subsided.

We headed down the stairs and out into the plaza where we'd eaten dinner the prior evening. It was "market day," and the place had been transformed—filled with vendors selling all types of clothing. We walked down a narrow street which opened to another plaza. It, too, had been converted into a market, selling fruits and vegetables. People were everywhere —shopping, eating, and talking.

I looked up to see what the weather gods had in store for us.

Marty was right—the sky was a flawless fluorescent blue. The temperature was in the 60s and was expected to peak at around 80 degrees in the afternoon. Perfect cycling weather.

We made our way to the Iglesia de San Miguel (Church of St. Michael), built in the 12th century, with a carved doorway depicting scenes of St. Michael the Archangel. From the side of the church, we had a sweeping view of the hills and landscape surrounding Estella.

Iglesia de San Miguel, Estella

We crossed a stone bridge over the river Ega, then climbed the steps of the 13th century Iglesia de San Pedro (St. Peter) de la Rua, the largest church in town. Inside, there were only two other people, plus an elderly man in the back—the caretaker. It was dimly lit and smelled of must and candles. Marty and I walked along the side aisles, stopping briefly in each of the ornately-decorated chapels. Near the main altar was a wooden carving of St. Peter. We sat down in silence for a few minutes.

After seeing the cathedral in Pamplona—and now these churches in Estella—we were becoming overwhelmed with the stunning architecture and detail of these enormous houses of worship. There would be 934 more churches to visit between here and Santiago. We'd need to pace ourselves.

We asked the caretaker to stamp our passports on our way out. Once outside, we saw a massive building across from the church which we hadn't noticed before. This was the Palace of the Kings and Queens of Navarre, an imposing fortress with arched wooden doorways, used for 300 years starting in the 12th century.

In front of the palace was a man in his seventies on an e-bike, with huge panniers attached to the back. We took a chance that we might communicate with him.

"*Hola!* Are you riding the Camino?" Marty asked.

"Yes, I certainly am," he replied in a British accent.

"We're Jim and Marty. Are you from the U.K.?"

"I'm Edward," he said, extending his hand. "From London. Started in St. Jean Pied de Port."

"Heading all the way to Santiago?" I asked.

"Yes, I am riding to Santiago, and then on to Cape Finisterre. I lost my wife last year—I'm going to spread her ashes into the Atlantic. And then I'm riding back to St. Jean."

"Oh, I'm sorry for your loss. But what a nice way to remember her," offered Marty.

"That's quite a ride, a thousand miles round-trip, right?" I said. "We haven't seen anyone going the other direction so far."

"I'm sure I'll get some looks," said Edward.

"Did you ride up the Hill of Forgiveness yesterday?"

"I did indeed. It was a challenge, and I walked a fair bit. Did you gents see that coffee-bus at the top?"

"Yes, but we didn't go inside," said Marty.

"Well, they have some benches and tables in there. I was sitting at one, drinking coffee, when the owner—a German—came over to me and said 'I need to get under your pants.'"

We looked at him, our eyebrows raised.

Edward continued, "I said 'Excuse me?' He repeated, 'I need

to get under your pants! Stand up!' So I stood up. Then, he reached over to the bench where I was sitting and pulled on it. Turns out there was a cupboard underneath the seat where he stores his coffee. I was relieved, of course."

"Darn, we missed that. Are you staying in albergues? Or hotels?" I asked.

"Albergues. Doing it cheap. Last night the room was full— twelve of us sleeping there. It was a bit noisy as I got into bed, and it took a while to fall asleep. But this morning I got up at five-thirty, and it was dark and silent. I thought I was the first one up. I looked around—it took me a minute to realize everyone else had already left! The walkers like to get going early."

"Well, we gotta get going too, Edward," I said. "Riding to Logroño today. Great to meet you—Buen Camino!"

"Buen Camino, gents!"

We returned to our apartment, packed our bags, and brought our bikes down the stairs. Once outside, we took in one more view of the bustling market in the plaza. We looked around but couldn't find a Camino marker. Marty approached a Spanish man who was browsing hats.

"Hey-o, señorit-o, which-o way-o Camino?" he asked in his improvised Spanglish.

He pointed toward the main street on the other side of the plaza. We rode over to it, found a waymark, and began pedaling out of town. Soon we were on the gravel Camino path on our way to Logroño.

A FEW MILES OUTSIDE ESTELLA, we saw a group of people on the side of the Camino, gathered in front of a stone wall. On the wall was a sign—"*Fuente del Vino*." We stopped, and I looked it up using my Translate app. It was a wine fountain!

We were at the start of the La Rioja wine region, and this

was the Bodegas Irache winery. The fountain was built in 1991
—on the 100th anniversary of the winery—and free Rioja has
been flowing for pilgrims ever since. There was a spigot on the
wall, and everyone was helping themselves.

The sign above the fountain was in Spanish. I used my app
to translate—it read:

> IF YOU WANT TO ARRIVE IN SANTIAGO WITH
> THE STRENGTH AND VITALITY OF THIS GREAT WINE,
> HAVE A DRINK AND TOAST TO HAPPINESS.

Even though it was still morning in Spain, it had to be five
o'clock somewhere. Why not?

There were no cups, so the pilgrims were improvising. One
woman was slurping wine with her scallop shell. A Frenchman
had taken the cap off his water bottle and was using it to take
tiny sips. Marty thought for a moment, then dumped all the
water out of his second bottle and filled it up with wine. If he
got stranded on the Camino, parched and dehydrated, at least
he would be relaxed.

Marty turning water into wine at the Bodegas Irache
fountain

After a few sips, we got back on our bikes. The Camino took us along rolling hills, with rock walls in the distance that resembled Utah. The landscape transitioned into La Rioja, and we passed vineyards, olive groves, apple trees, and lots of other agriculture. It looked like Napa or Sonoma Valley.

Marty and I cruised along, enjoying the scenery.

"Jumbo, that's some trip Edward is doing, huh?"

"Yeah, it's probably easier on an e-bike, but still—a thousand miles all by himself. Sounds like he's processing a lot, bringing his wife's ashes."

"Like Martin Sheen in the movie," said Marty.

"Hey Marty, I know I'm gonna be around for at least another twenty years... maybe thirty, like we talked about. But in the off chance that something should happen to me on this trip... you know, and I don't make it... I want you to finish it."

"Whoa, Jumbo!" Marty said laughing. "That's not gonna happen!"

"Well, you never know, it could." I was chuckling too. "And if it did, I want you to carry my ashes with you, like Edward. Sprinkle them into the ocean."

"Jumbo, that's not happening. Besides, you know I'm going first."

"But if it did?"

"Okay, if it did, I would do that. You have my word." Marty thought for another moment. "How would I carry your ashes?"

I looked over at the two water bottles attached to his frame.

"Dump the wine out and put my ashes in there."

"Okay Jumbo, got it. And I hope you'd do the same for me if, you know, I somehow don't make it."

"Of course. Your ashes in my water bottle, same deal."

Marty paused, looked down at his belly, and then at my water bottle.

"You're gonna need a bigger bottle."

16

THE LOST MARTY
ESTELLA TO LOS ARCOS

W ine was first made sometime around 6000 BC, in what is now Georgia in Eastern Europe. By 1000 BC, the Phoenicians had turned winemaking and trading into an industry, bringing wine to other regions in the ancient Mediterranean. Pretty much every civilization since then has found increasingly more efficient ways to convert grape juice into a fruity booze. Today, mass production has enabled winemaking to become a $500 billion global industry. With over 500 wineries and 16,000 grape growers, La Rioja in Spain is part of that machine.

When you think of big industries, you think of smokestacks and assembly lines. Forests being cleared. Oceans being polluted. Few industries actually seem to *improve* on what nature created. To me, winemaking is one of them.

As we rode along the Camino, we passed one vineyard after another, stitched perfectly into the hillsides. Long rows of grapevines hugged the gentle slopes, their gnarled branches resting on rustic wooden trellises. The shiny, green, spider-veined leaves were tinged with red at this time of year, with yearning tendrils reaching toward the sun. The grapes... well...

they looked like grapes. Do I really need to come up with a fancy way of describing them?

I mean, come on, grapevines are downright gorgeous! The vines had turned an otherwise barren landscape into a thing of beauty. It's almost as if they were planted intentionally for our viewing pleasure.

Vineyards in La Rioja

While they are lovely to look at, there is one thing that grapevines aren't good for—shade. Although the day's clear sky made for stunning views, by noontime, Marty and would have easily traded it for some cloud cover. But we didn't want to complain too much—we knew there would be rainy days ahead.

Rounding a bend, we spied a large grove of trees up ahead. As we approached, we realized they were olive trees. The green fruit were everywhere—hanging just below the silvery leaves.

Olive grove near Los Arcos

We ducked under a tree. Now shielded from the sun, we drank from our water bottles and took another sip of Marty's wine. Unfortunately, the olives weren't yet ripe—they would have paired perfectly with the Rioja.

"Can you believe this, Jumbo? Pinch yourself. We're riding our bikes in Spain!"

Olive tree

Suddenly, with no advance warning, we were attacked by a swarm of mosquitoes. It was a full-on coordinated ambush, as if they were laying in wait in the olive grove, prepared to launch an attack on any unsuspecting pilgrim who dared take cover there. Instead of biting our exposed arms and legs—which would have been easy for these bloodsucking marauders—the assault was focused on our thighs, biting right through our Spandex riding shorts. Our only guess was that they were attracted to the anti-chafe cream we had lathered inside, and since they hadn't seen any humans in a while, it was "go time."

"Let's get outta here!" said Marty. We scrambled to get on our bikes and started pedaling hard, steering with one hand and swatting with the other.

Once we'd escaped the onslaught, scratching at our welts, we passed an apple orchard. Marty picked one and ate it—it perked him up and took his mind off the bites for a while. We also passed vast fields of red pepper plants, with workers stooped over in the hot sun harvesting the ripe vegetables.

The trail was dry, and we left a cloud of dust as we rode through vineyards and farms. Our legs were pumping, and we were puffing. At one point, I thought I detected a slight whiff of manure. On my next deep inhale, I knew I was right.

Where was it coming from? We looked to our right and got our answer—it was a bull farm! We wondered whether these creatures would someday be part of an encierro, running in Pamplona or one of the other nearby towns.

About ten miles into our ride from Estella, we heard a man's voice from behind us. This was a first—so far, we'd been moving faster than all the pilgrims we'd seen on the trail.

"Buen Camino!" he called out.

I pulled in single-file behind Marty. A man in his forties on a mountain bike blazed past us, kicking up dirt behind him.

One thing to know about Marty is that he doesn't like to be passed by another rider. He takes it as a personal challenge and pedals as hard as he can to catch up. Like a dog chasing a car, Marty took off after him. I kept my easy pace and let them go.

After another mile, the trail began a long ascent, and the surface condition worsened. There were loose rocks with a deep rut in the middle—it felt like the Hill of Forgiveness all over again. I looked ahead and saw Marty and the other rider stopped on the side of the Camino. I joined them, and together we assessed the situation.

His name was Francis, from Belgium, and he was riding to Santiago alone. He spoke English, and we debated whether to stay on the Camino or turn around and get on the road. Francis wanted to keep going, but Marty and I decided to backtrack toward the last village, where we recalled seeing a road heading off to the side. We bid him farewell and a "Buen Camino."

Whenever you see a pilgrim heading in the opposite direction on the Camino, something's usually wrong. They must be lost, or they're injured, or they really need a beer and decided the next town was too far. It's not normal. As Marty and I made our way back to the village, several pilgrims gave us a curious look, not sure whether to say "Buen Camino" or ask if we were okay. We spared them the awkwardness and initiated the greeting ourselves.

We arrived at the hilltop village, which was deserted. I opened Google Maps and punched in "Los Arcos," the next town along the way to Logroño. Google immediately found a route which would put us on a paved road to Los Arcos, now less than five miles away.

"Follow me," I said to Marty. He nodded.

I began pedaling through the settlement with Marty behind me. There were a number of side streets, and Google had me make several turns.

"Once we get through this village, we should be in Los Arcos in half an hour," I said. "Good timing for a lunch stop."

Marty didn't respond, which was unusual. I looked over my shoulder. He was gone.

I stopped my bike and turned around.

"Marty!"

Silence.

"Marty!!" I yelled as loud as I could. "Where are you?!"

Still nothing. I tried calling his cell phone, but there was no answer. I retraced my path and rode back through the town.

"Marty!!"

No Marty. In fact, no one at all. I went down several side streets calling his name but couldn't find him. How could I have lost him in this little town, so quickly? I was getting worried.

Just then, a woman appeared on a street corner and motioned to me. She silently pointed down a street I hadn't yet searched. I pedaled down the road, turned right, and there was Marty. I looked back to thank her, but she was gone—our Camino Angel #2.

"What happened?" I asked. "You were right behind me!"

"Yeah, I stopped to take a picture, and when I looked up, you were gone."

"Sorry about that. From now on I'll watch more closely. Gotta keep you alive—can't afford to lose you."

Marty snickered. "Jumbo, it's gonna be kinda hard to lose me out here. I'm literally the biggest guy in Spain on a bike."

17

THE "OTHER ME"
LOS ARCOS TO LOGROÑO

The year was 1067. King Sancho the Great, ruler of most of northern Spain until his death in 1035, had left behind three grandsons—all first cousins—to run sections of his divided kingdom. All three were named "Sancho."

Sancho II controlled Castile, Sancho IV governed Navarre, and Sancho Ramirez led Aragon. Even though these kingdoms were quite large, each of them wanted more, and they were willing to fight for it. The fact that they were related didn't seem to matter.

After a few skirmishes, the family rivalry came to a head in a tiny village on the river Odron on the western edge of Navarre, in Sancho IV's territory. The town had been relatively peaceful for over a century, ever since the Christians wrested it from the Moors in 914. That was about to change.

Fighting erupted in August 1067 in what became known as the "War of the Three Sanchos." Realizing a three-way battle was like playing whack-a-mole, Sancho IV and Sancho Ramirez formed an alliance. When Sancho II approached the small village, Sancho IV's archers mounted a stiff defense, fending off the attacking cousin and retaining the settlement as part of Navarre.

King Sancho IV was so impressed with his archers that he placed two bows and arrows on the village's coat of arms, giving rise to its name—*Los Arcos*—meaning "the bows."

As Marty and I rode into Los Arcos, we saw no evidence of all this bloodshed. It's a small, quaint Camino town with a population of less than 1,200. In the center, a cobbled plaza graces the front of the village's crown jewel, the Iglesia de Santa Maria. On this beautiful day, the plaza was filled with pilgrims sitting outside having lunch.

We got our passports stamped and ordered some food at the bar—eggs and potatoes for Marty, paella for me. Most of the tables were taken, but we spotted two empty chairs at a table where a couple was seated.

"Hola," I said. "Can... we... uh... join you?" *I really wished I'd learned some Spanish.*

"Of course," replied the man in perfect English.

They were Americans—the first we'd met since we arrived in Spain. Derek had studied computer science at Carnegie Mellon University (Marty's alma mater) in Pittsburgh. His wife, Alice, was also a computer scientist. Recently retired, they were taking 35 days to walk the Camino together.

"Do you have a plan of where you are staying each night, or are you letting it flow?" I asked.

Alice looked at Derek and giggled. "Show him your spreadsheet, honey."

Derek grinned and pulled out a multi-page spreadsheet, bound in a folder with a cover on the front and back.

I nodded with approval. "Impressive."

Marty rolled his eyes. "Jumbo, show him yours."

I produced my laminated sheet. We all laughed. I had found the "other me," a kindred spirit on the Camino.

The "Other Me" in Los Arcos

At the next table sat three women with ice bags on their knees and bandages on their feet. We introduced ourselves, and they reciprocated—Annika from Sweden, Emily from Vancouver and Vivian from Dublin.

"How long have you been walking?" Marty asked.

"About a week," said Annika. "We all met near Roncesvalles in the Pyrenees."

"Looks like it's been tough already," I said, pointing at their legs. "We saw a bunch of people yesterday on the Hill of Forgiveness with sprained ankles and blisters."

"It's harder on the way down than on the way up with these heavy packs," said Emily.

"You guys are biking, eh?" asked Vivian. "No blisters, I guess?" They all laughed.

"Well, that is true," I said, feeling a little guilty. "My back is hurting a little, but the feet are fine."

"What made you guys decide to cycle the Camino?" asked Emily.

"We both retired recently and were looking for a new adventure together. How about you all?"

"Vivian and I each lost a parent over the last year," said Emily. "Needed some time to work things out."

"I'm sorry," said Marty.

"Being with other people going through the same thing really helps," said Vivian, looking at Emily.

Just then, a cyclist pulled into the plaza. It was Francis from Belgium, who had made his way to Los Arcos on the rocky, rutty Camino trail we'd abandoned earlier. We asked him how it was.

"Very bad," he said. "Lots of loose rocks—I went down hard just past where I left you." He showed us the scrapes on his leg. Marty and I were glad we'd taken the road.

We finished our lunches, bid "Buen Camino" to all the pilgrims we'd just met, and got back on the trail towards Logroño.

18

THE COJONUDO
LOGROÑO

The seventeen miles from Los Arcos to Logroño were challenging, yet serene and beautiful, as we continued to pass vineyards and farms on both sides of the Camino. It was still very hot. Once we finished the wine, we stopped to refill our bottles at one of the potable water fountains which appear frequently along the path.

Just outside Logroño, we passed what looked like cliff dwellings set high in the hill to the right. Several rectangular windows were carved into the sand-colored, striated rock.

Mount Cantabria, near Logroño

This was Mount Cantabria, a settlement inhabited by the Berones, a Celt-Iberian people who occupied La Rioja in ancient times before the Romans arrived here in the first century BC.

Over two thousand years later, Logroño is all about wine. As the capital of La Rioja, Logroño is a relatively large city (in Camino terms) with over 150,000 residents. Many of the big Rioja labels are headquartered here—Marques de Murrieta, Campo Viejo, and lots of others.

The path routed us along the Ebro river and into the city center, where we found an outdoor café across from the Logroño Cathedral. We had ridden about 30 miles with 1,900 feet of climbing. With the rough surface, it felt like twice that. We had 390 miles to go to Santiago. It was time for a beer.

Logroño Cathedral

"Jumbo, nice work." Marty raised his glass as we toasted to our second day on the Camino. We took our first sips.

Marty set down his beer and stared at it. He squinted his eyes. "Jumbo, why is beer so good?"

"You mean—what *makes* it so good? Well, I don't know, probably the way the barley is toasted, the hops..." The engineer in me was attempting to analyze this glorious, sudsy substance at a molecular level.

Marty closed his eyes, as if in some sort of meditative trance. "No, I mean... *why* is beer *so good?*"

I thought for a moment. "Are you saying you wish beer *wasn't* so good, so you didn't want it all the time?" I chuckled.

It was as if he hadn't heard me. "Jumbo." Marty now opened his eyes and looked directly at me. "W*hy* is beer so good?"

At this point, I realized this was one of Marty's philosophical questions that only someone with a lot of free time would be pondering. And he wasn't really looking for an answer.

I gave him one anyway. "I don't know, Marty, it just *is*. It's like it *knows* where in your body it needs to go. It's working its way into my lower back and quads right now."

"Yeah, same with me! It's heading to my butt and calves today. How does it *do* that?"

"It's just really smart. It must have artificial intelligence."

Calle de Laurel, Logroño

With this deep question still unanswered, we finished our beers and walked our bikes through the town to our Airbnb. It was in the heart of Calle de Laurel, an area known for great tapas. There were over 50 tapas bars within four blocks of our apartment, and two of them were directly below.

Marty and I cleaned up and headed out. All the tapas restaurants were open air, with display cases showing their offerings. One place caught our eye—its case held a dozen biscuits with chorizo and a quail egg on top, called the *Cojonudo*. I looked it up—the word is slang for "F$%#'ing Great." It's also the name of a special tapas which is local to the region. With a name like that, how could we pass it up? We went inside and found a table.

Cojonudo

I stepped up to the bar and ordered a Cojonudo, along with two other tapas—meatballs and bacala. Within seconds, the meatballs and fish arrived. We quickly demolished them and anxiously awaited the Cojonudo. We looked at the bartender— he was standing behind the bar talking to one of his co-workers. The case was still full of Cojonudos, but he hadn't yet pulled one out for us.

Thinking he may have forgotten about it, I walked over to him and pointed at the Cojonudo, adding a *"Por favor?"* He nodded. I went back to our table, watching him as he stood there, continuing to talk to his friend.

We sat patiently, still hungry, waiting for the tapas to arrive. The bartender then took two Cojonudos from the case and put them in a small oven. Marty and I looked at each other, smiling and nodding. Surely one of them was coming our way.

After a minute, he removed the hot tapas, put them on two plates, and headed toward us. Without making eye contact with us, he walked by and served them to a couple at the next table. As they began eating them, the look on their faces said it all—"F$%#'ing Great!"

This time, Marty stepped up to the bar and pointed to the Cojonudo case.

"Sí," said the bartender, nodding.

Still, nothing happened. The man picked up a towel and started drying beer glasses. Marty and I were getting frustrated —this was decidedly *not* F$%#'ing Great.

"Do you think this is something they do to mess with Americans?" Marty asked. "First, they give the thing a name that makes it sound irresistible. Then they take your order and tell you it's coming. And then they make you wait—and ask *again?* And again?"

"Yeah, and all the while they're bringing Cojonudos right and left to everyone else, but not to the Americans." I added. "That's gotta be what's going on here. It's pure torture."

"I think everyone's in on it," Marty said. "They all know we want it. That couple there, look at them, how happy they are. The bartender set those Cojonudos down where we can see them—and smell them—but we can't have them."

"Yeah. I'd love one, but it's not worth waiting." I said. "Let's head out." We paid our bill, got our passports stamped and walked out into the street. The elusive Cojonudo would have to wait for our next trip to Spain.

We stopped at another tapas bar and met three Americans —John, Shannon, and Lorraine. John was from Indianapolis, and Shannon and Lorraine were from Washington State. The trio had hiked 20 miles together that day.

This was John's third year in a row on the Camino—he'd been gone the whole month of September the last three years. He said that by the end of the month, his grandkids start to wonder if they'll ever see him again.

This year, John was doing something different. He had walked from St. Jean Pied de Port to Logroño, where he had rented a bike. He planned to start riding it the next morning from Logroño to León, where he would return it and then walk the rest of the way to Santiago. Marty and I had never considered this option and were very intrigued.

After a pleasant chat, we said farewell, headed back to our apartment, and turned in around 11:00 p.m. After a long day on the trail, we were ready for some shut-eye.

19

THE HOT SPARE
LOGROÑO

I had just dozed off when, around midnight, I was jolted awake by the sound of loud music and people singing, talking, and shouting. It sounded like a giant dance party was raging underneath my bed. Apparently, the folks in Logroño liked to cut loose on Thursday nights (and possibly every night), and they continued partying below us into the wee hours of the morning.

I tossed and turned, scratching at my mosquito bites. My back was aching—the cumulative effect of two days of bumpy riding. I lay awake, worrying about how I could manage the 45-mile ride to Belorado, our next destination, while sleep-deprived and in pain. At around 4:00 a.m., with the music still blasting, I gave up trying to sleep and walked out to the living room.

Coffee, I thought. Might as well get the coffee started. I located the coffee maker but couldn't find any coffee in our apartment. I opened up every cabinet—no sign of the stuff. I'd need to wait until the cafés opened for an espresso.

I LOVE ESPRESSO. How and when did that happen? Actually, I didn't start drinking coffee until I was in my early thirties. Somehow I made it through college, grad school, and the first two years of fatherhood without java. When our second son was born in 1994, the sleepless nights were wearing on me, so I began drinking coffee with lots of milk and sugar. Within two months, I was drinking it black. And two months after that, I switched to straight espresso, a habit I have retained to this day.

A daily espresso habit essentially requires that one have a home espresso machine. In the mid-1990s, Starbucks sold a machine—the "Barista"—which produced an excellent shot of espresso with a perfect layer of crema on top. I bought one and immediately started using it every day. It was bright blue—Katie and I nicknamed it "The Big Blue Beast."

One weekend when Belle and Marty were visiting us in Maryland, I fired up the Beast and made cappuccinos for everyone. Marty enjoyed it so much that he bought a Barista machine for himself when he got back to Pittsburgh. He began making a cappuccino every day before heading off to work.

Four years later, Big Blue broke down. I sent it in to have it repaired and had to wait a month, only to learn that it was too far gone. At the end of that very difficult espressoless period, I ended up shelling out $400 for a new one.

On our next trip to Pittsburgh the following summer, Marty was making cappuccinos with his Barista machine, and we sat on his porch enjoying them. His son, Sam, was there as well. As usual, Marty had lost track of days and was very relaxed.

As Marty began making one for Sam, the unthinkable happened: his Barista machine stopped working. Marty immediately placed a call to Starbucks. Based on his description of the problem, they told him it likely could not be repaired.

Sam was bummed. Marty, however, didn't break a sweat.

"Sam, not to worry. Follow me," he said calmly. He then motioned to me. "Jumbo, come check this out."

Sam and I followed Marty into his garage. There were many shelves stacked with camping gear, cases of beer, and biking accessories. Marty pushed aside an old tent and Coleman stove to reveal a box tucked in behind. I peered in and immediately recognized it—a brand new Starbucks Barista machine, still in its original packaging.

"Is that what I think it is?" I asked.

"Yes it is, Jumbo. Once I saw what happened to you when your machine broke down, I decided to look for a spare 'just in case.' I got it on eBay. It was a great deal—only $100."

Marty is not much of a planner, but when it comes to things at the physiological level of Marty's Hierarchy of Needs—beer, junk food, coffee, shade, and chairs—he does plan ahead.

"Well, Marty, this explains a lot," I said.

"What?"

"You're looking even more relaxed than usual these days, and now I know why."

"What do you mean?"

"Well, buried deep in your subconsciousness is the knowledge that you have this hot spare. And at any given time, if your Barista gives out, you know you can just go into the garage, pull out this spare, and put it into service. Like what happened just now. You'll never miss a day. I think it gives you a certain inner peace. Am I right?"

Sam was beside himself. "You have a *spare* cappuccino machine?! Lemme get this straight, Marty. We get paper IOUs for Christmas because you don't have time to shop, but you had time to buy yourself an *extra coffee maker* as a backup?"*

---

* Marty gives his children paper IOU's as Christmas presents—printed in color—because his busy schedule does not allow time for him to buy actual presents. He also claims that giving IOU's is better than giving actual gifts because "When you give a physical gift, it's over as soon as they open it. This way they have the added joy of anticipating it over multiple days."

Also, as mentioned earlier, Marty's children call him by his first name.

"Well, Sam, that's true. But think about it—who benefits from this today? *You,* that's who! Let me boot this thing up, and you'll be drinking a cappuccino within ten minutes."

Once Marty's hot spare was in service, he quickly got on eBay and bought another one. To this day, Marty still has a spare in his garage. And he still gives IOUs for Christmas.

BACK IN LOGROÑO, in desperate need of an espresso, I checked the time. It was 5:30 a.m. and still dark outside.

After another hour, Marty came out of his room.

"Did you get any sleep?" I asked.

"Not much," he said, rubbing his eyes. "That was some party down there last night."

"Yeah, they were going till after four," I said. "I think I may have slept an hour, if that. And my back is hurting pretty bad. I'm really not sure I can ride today."

Marty pondered the situation. "Jumbo, let's not make any decisions until we have some espresso and pastries."

Obviously, I agreed. We got dressed, headed outside, found a café, and sipped on our espressos as we discussed several alternatives. We decided that renting a car would be the best solution. With a car, I could drive while Marty rode his bike to Belorado, or we could drive together and take the day off.

We decided on the second option. Using my phone, I reserved a car with Avis online. It was now 9:00 a.m., and the confirmation email said the car was ready to be picked up.

We finished our breakfast and walked more than a mile to the car rental facility. When we arrived, the door was padlocked with a chain across the handles. A placard listing the office's hours indicated they opened at 8:30 a.m. We peered inside—it was dark. *Where were they?*

Just then, Marty spotted a handwritten note on the door:

VOLVEREMOS PRONTO
(WE'LL BE BACK SOON)

It also listed a phone number. I quickly called it.

"Ho-la." It was a man's voice, sounding groggy, as if I'd woken him from a deep sleep.

"Habla Inglés?" I asked.

He cleared his throat. "Yes."

"We're at the Avis building. I reserved a car for today."

"Ah...you did? Okay, I'll be there soon."

We waited about fifteen minutes, with still no sign of anyone. Marty pointed at a sign on the wall of the building. It had the Avis logo and their motto: "We Try Harder."

"Harder than who? Rip Van Winkle?" Marty snickered.

Finally, the Avis attendant came walking down the street, twirling a lanyard, his hair tousled and his clothes wrinkled. He unlocked the door, removed the chain, and led us inside.

He tapped on his computer and found our reservation. Next, he asked for my international driver's license. *Who thought I'd be driving on this trip?* I told him I didn't have one.

"Sorry, it's a requirement. We can't rent the car without it."

My back was in pain, and I was operating on no sleep. Just then, another idea popped into my head.

"Bus?" I asked the attendant.

"Sí," he said, and pointed toward the bus station. It was another half-mile walk. We thanked him and set off.

Arriving at the bus station, we learned there were no buses to Belorado, our planned destination for the day. However, there were several buses to Burgos, our next stop after Belorado. By taking the bus, we would miss a 75-mile stretch of the Camino. But we would have two nights and an entire day in Burgos, a large city with lots to see. We decided to take the 5:30 p.m. bus to Burgos.

That gave us the afternoon to do some "chillin'" in Logroño.

At this point we had eaten almost no vegetables, so we found a tapas place that served gazpacho. The cold soup was refreshing, and we each slurped down two bowls. We then sat on a bench and people-watched for a few hours, while we negated the health benefits of our gazpacho with more pastries—and cervezas. The name of the pastry shop was *El Paraiso,* which means "Paradise." We agreed they were heavenly.

El Paraiso pastry shop in Logroño

Finally, it was time to head to the bus station. When we

arrived, the bus driver told us that our bikes needed to go in the luggage hold, and we needed to remove the wheels. Marty stooped down and climbed into the luggage compartment as I fed him the bikes, piece by piece.

While Marty was still inside the hold, precisely at 5:30 p.m., the driver started closing the luggage door on him.

"Stop! Please!" I yelled to the driver, but the door kept closing. Having already paid for a nonrefundable seat for Marty, I was eager to get him out of there. He stuck out his arm and stopped the door, just before he was trapped inside.

We boarded the bus and began a two-hour drive along the "asphalt Camino." Looking out the window, I saw the highway signs indicating the towns we would have ridden through— Najera, Santo Domingo de la Calzada, Belorado, and San Juan de Ortega. I felt some pangs of regret knowing we wouldn't get to see them.

Once we arrived in Burgos, we reassembled our bikes in the station, turned on our headlights, and rode to our Airbnb in the dark. We immediately went to bed without dinner. I was exhausted and drifted off quickly.

20

HUMAN EVOLUTION
BURGOS

T he next morning, we arose in Burgos and made coffee.

"Marty, I haven't asked, but I know we're well outside your thirty-mile radius. All good in that department?"

"Well, Jumbo, I gotta be honest, since that first day in Pamplona—you know, the one that didn't count—nada."

I counted the days on my fingers. Pamplona, Estella, Logroño, Burgos...

"Yowza."

"Yeah, it's not fun. But really, the whole situation actually benefits you," said Marty.

"How?" I couldn't see the connection.

"Think about it. Have you had to wait to use the bathroom in the morning over the past week? Even once? It's been all yours, right?"

I grinned and nodded. As I sipped my coffee, I looked out our window. We were on the third floor, and our view faced west, toward the *meseta*, Spanish for "tabletop" or "plateau." It was a wide open, treeless landscape that seemed to go on forever, with wheat fields and a line of windmills that dissolved into the horizon. It had a foreboding look that appeared even more ominous with the gray sky above.

That would be our challenge for tomorrow. But today, we were in Burgos, and for one day we didn't need to worry about our bikes. We left them in the room, went down the stairs, opened the front door, and were immediately captivated by the city.

Burgos is steeped in history, some of which parallels that of Logroño and Pamplona. The area was first inhabited by Celtic tribes, who were driven out by the Romans in the first century BC. Then came the Visigoths in the 400s, followed by the Moors in the early 700s. In the mid-800s, King Alfonso III the Great of León reconquered the city for Spain and built several castles, primarily to defend Christendom against the Moors.

In the 11th century, Burgos became the capital of the Kingdom of Castile, the wealthiest and most powerful kingdom in Spain in the Middle Ages (Castile's capital later moved to Toledo and then to Granada when Ferdinand and Isabella came on the scene in the 1400s). The growth in the number of pilgrims on the Camino added to the affluence of this royal city.

In addition to the Moorish invasion, Burgos has seen its share of other wars—with nearby rival Spanish kingdoms, with Napoleonic France, and between the Republicans and Nationalists in the Spanish Civil War in the 1930s.

Today, Burgos is a thriving city with a population of 180,000. As we toured the city center, Burgos' legacy of power and wealth was evident everywhere—in impressive churches, monasteries, plazas, and its stunning riverwalk along the Arlanzón River.

Marty and I stopped in a café and got some pastries and espressos. As we'd decided in Logroño, no major decisions were to be made without them. While we ate, we began mapping out our day. My back was feeling a little better, and I was up for doing some walking. We agreed we would aim to see the Museum of Human Evolution, the Monastery de las Huel-gas, the Burgos Cathedral, and the Castle.

We made our way to the museum and arrived as it was opening. It was a fascinating place. In the late 1990s, just outside Burgos in the village of Atapuerca, archeologists discovered caves with the remains of over 5,500 human skeletons dating as far back as 1.2 million years.

Tools used by Homo Antecessor, found in caves near Burgos

These were the first hominids in Western Europe—*Homo Antecessor*. The evolutionary lines of the African ancestors of modern humans have been traced by the findings in this site. Archeologists learned that these hominids hunted using fabricated tools and even had a traditional burial culture. On the walls of the caves, they found painted and engraved panels depicting animals and hunting scenes. They also learned that they were sometimes cannibalistic.

"Jumbo, what would drive a person to eat another person?"

"I don't know. I mean, they clearly hunted animals, so they did have other sources of meat."

"It must have been more of a back-up strategy. Like... when unexpected guests would come over and stay for dinner."

"Yeah, I can see that one—that woman there—saying to her husband in the kitchen, 'How are we gonna feed all these people?' And the husband would be like... 'Well, what about Johnny?'"

We were cracking up. Everyone else in the place seemed very serious, and we were attracting some disapproving looks.

"Looks like they had a tough life, huh, Jumbo?"

"Yeah, and to think we're descended from them."

"Speak for yourself," said Marty.

"You don't think you evolved from these?" I couldn't tell where Marty was going with this.

"I don't know, these people worked pretty hard. Making tools, hunting, eating each other. None of the wall paintings shows them sitting down. It doesn't look like a lot of 'chillin' was going on. I don't see anything I have in common with them."

Now I understood his tack. "Right. There must have been another branch of hominid somewhere that was more advanced—the *Homo Marty*. With an entire museum dedicated to human evolution, I'm surprised there's no mention of it."

The museum also included a section on Charles Darwin and his work on natural selection and evolution from the 1800s, with a focus on his expedition to South America and the Galápagos Islands. Katie and I had a trip planned to the Galápagos the following February, so this especially interested me.

Our next stop was the Monastery de las Huelgas, a convent which is still active and holds the tombs of Kings and Queens from the Middle Ages. In those days, over 100 nuns lived here; today they number 23. We had to wait a few minutes for our tour to begin, so we stepped into the courtyard and looked around.

"Jumbo, you know what's missing here?"

"Shade?"

"Well, that's true, but what else?"

I ventured a second guess. "Beer?"

"Well... yes, but that's not what I was thinking."

"Chairs!"

"Yes! Benches! Not a single bench in this entire courtyard."

It never occurred to me to look for a place to sit for just a few minutes, but for Marty, it was the first and only thing on his mind.

Monastery de las Huelgas. Where are the benches?

The monastery was vast. We walked through the the royal tombs, the church, the cloister, and the grounds. The tour was in Spanish, but the guide took a few minutes after each stop to give Marty and me a quick summary in English.

Inside one chapel, we saw a shocking sculpture. It was a depiction of St. James on a horse with three Moors being trampled underneath. Thus far along the Camino, we had seen statues and paintings of St. James depicted in other ways—typically as a pilgrim or teacher. This was the first time we had seen *Santiago Matamoros,* or "St. James the Moor Slayer," and we would see it repeatedly during the remainder of our time along the Camino.

St. James Matamoros (the "Moor Slayer")

The image dates back to the year 844, when the Christian army was outnumbered and nearly defeated in a battle against the Moors near Clavijo, just south of Logroño. St. James is said to have appeared on a white horse, sword in hand, leading the Christians to an upset victory. The story spread across Spain, with St. James becoming known as the hero of the Reconquest. From that point forward, he was revered as the country's patron saint, and the image became a unifying force for Christians as they fought the Moors over the next six centuries.

"Looks like St. James is taking out some Moops up there," commented Marty.

"Yeah, three at a time. They don't look too happy."

We left the monastery and walked over to the centerpiece of Burgos—the Cathedral of Santa Maria. Patterned after Notre Dame in Paris, it is massive and every bit as ornate as its parent in France. Inside, we visited all fifteen of its chapels, each one with impressive detail. I sat and said a prayer of thanks for the trip and this day.

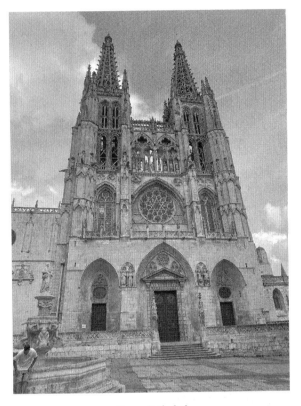

Burgos Cathedral

We got our passports stamped, then left the cathedral and hiked up to the grounds of the old castle at the top of the city. The castle was blown up by the French as they moved out of town after losing the war with the Spanish in the 1800s. It was closed due to construction, but the view from the top of the hill was spectacular.

We ended the day at a café on the plaza across from the cathedral, and soon our cervezas arrived along with some Spanish olives. While all key decisions on this trip were being made over espresso and pastries, we found that the processing and debriefing of each day occurred best over cervezas.

Processing and debriefing in Burgos

We looked around the plaza and gazed at the grand façade of the church. Marty broke the silence.

"Jumbo, don't you find it interesting that these people in the Middle Ages spent so much time and money building these enormous cathedrals and monasteries—all to honor God—and then along comes Darwin in the 1800s and turns it all upside down with his theory?"

Only a few sips into our first beer of the day, Marty had suddenly made a ninety-degree departure from our typical adolescent banter. This was heavy stuff. The Camino must have been working on him.

"Where did that come from, Marty?"

"I don't know, the museum and the cathedral tour today got me thinking."

"Well, I guess I never really thought about it that way."

"You're Catholic, Jumbo. But you're also an engineer and have a logical mind. What do *you* think?"

I paused for a moment.

"I really don't think the two are mutually exclusive. I mean, I believe in God, but I also believe in evolution."

"How does that work?" Marty popped an olive into his mouth and bit down. He winced. "Pits," he said as he spit out the hard center.

"I don't really think of the creation story in Genesis as completely factual. It's a story," I said. "I mean, I believe God created the universe and has a hand in everything. But I also believe humans evolved through natural selection. And he lets things happen because of our free will."

"That's what I struggle with, Jumbo. Why would God then let bad things happen to good people? You know, stuff like war, hunger, disease..."

Where do I go with this?

"That's a tough one, Marty. I don't know the answer. I think God has a hand in everything, but he lets us make choices and doesn't *stop* things from happening. It's like he set up the chess board but lets us play the game."

We were really getting into it now.

"But all these churches..."

I continued, "Well, about two thousand years ago, I think God decided we needed some help down here, so he upset the chess board a bit. He sent someone to show us how we're supposed to act. What I find amazing is how Jesus became so well-known—without TV, a blog, a YouTube channel or anything. His miracles, his message—they must have been compelling. Even some of the Romans converted. And over a thousand years later, in the Middle Ages, what he started was still going strong, and that's why they built these churches."

"Hmmm..."

"I think it's cool that the Camino we're on was part of this too. Millions of people have been inspired to walk hundreds of miles to visit the tomb of one of his apostles."

"But the whole idea of indulgences—the church even sold them, right?"

"Yeah, well, I don't know about that. There was definitely some weird stuff happening in the church over the centuries. I guess bad things can sometimes happen when you get people and money and power mixed together."

We both took another sip of our beers.

"Well, lots to think about out here, Jumbo. Good stuff." Marty raised his glass, and we toasted to a successful day and some solid introspection.

One of these is a stationary figure affixed to a bench. The other is a bronze statue. You decide which is which.

21

THE MESETA
BURGOS TO CASTROJERIZ

Burgos is the start of the meseta, the "tabletop." For the next 120 miles between Burgos and León, Marty and I would be riding on a relatively flat section with very little shade. Marty melts in the heat, so this was the section that most intimidated him.

We had decided we would attempt to conquer the meseta in two days, instead of the eight to ten days typically taken by pilgrims on foot. This would be our longest day of the trip thus far—55 miles. We had 307 miles to go to Santiago.

On a calm, warm, sunny day, there is nothing like riding a bike. Cruising along at an easy pace, you're creating your own gentle breeze, as if a fan were attached to your handlebars. The scenery changes at just the right pace compared to driving or walking—not too fast and not too slow. You're out in the open —your heightened senses see and smell everything; your ears are treated to the constant crackle of rubber on crushed gravel. It's impossible to use your phone while riding, so you're fully present and in the moment. Every few pedal strokes, you take a break and glide effortlessly. You're weightless—your joints don't hurt and your feet don't have blisters. You feel like a kid again.

On other days, biking is nothing like that. When Marty and I awoke in Burgos and gazed out our window, we knew we were in for a challenge. The sky was black, and the windmills were turning. That could only mean two things—rain and wind.

"Get ready to get wet, Jumbo."

Marty rides in all kids of weather—thunderstorms, snow, hail, you name it. He was undaunted. I, however, was most definitely daunted.

We put on our rain gear—lightweight rain shells, "waterproof" shorts, clear glasses, and covers over our helmets that looked like shower caps. I popped some Advil for my back.

Marty was watching me. "Let me carry your bike from now on," he said. "Don't strain yourself. We've got a long way to go."

He brought the bikes down the stairs, one-by-one. We rode to a convenience store to look for energy bars, but had to settle for Peanut M&Ms instead. Spotting a Camino marker, we began riding out of the city and into the meseta.

Pilgrims in rain gear starting on the meseta outside Burgos

Within ten minutes, it started sprinkling. Many pilgrims were out in their rain gear—we took it slowly to avoid splashing them. The drizzle soon turned into a driving rain.

The downpour pelted our bodies as we pedaled along. After a few wet miles, we stopped in a small village and ducked under the eave of a tiny church. We took stock—the water had already penetrated our shorts, shoes, and even our rain shells.

Water inside our rain shells? Calling these things rain shells would be an insult to rain shells worldwide. They were nearly worthless. But with no alternative, we kept them on.

With the rain continuing, we mounted our bikes and began a steady climb. As we crested the hilltop, countless miles of meseta lay before us. The brown plains were pocked with small dome-shaped mounds, similar to pictures I'd seen of the surface of Mars. Heavy gray clouds enshrouded the landscape in a gloomy half-light. We'd be riding across this entire expanse today. I was simultaneously awestruck and terrified.

The Meseta

Fully exposed to the deluge, we pressed on.

The path made a long descent into the village of Hornillos del Camino. Coasting downhill was a welcome relief to our thighs. But as our speed increased, the raindrops felt like needles hitting our faces, and we were creating our own windchill.

The Camino leveled out as we pedaled into the town. *Hornillos* means "stoves" or "ovens"—clay tiles and pottery were made here in the Middle Ages. In those days, three hospitals were also located here, two of which catered to pilgrims with leprosy. Only one hospital remains, and its leprosy wing has long since been decommissioned.

We stopped to get out of the rain and met many pilgrims doing the same. After a brief break and a passport stamp, we returned to the Camino. By this point, the temperature had dropped into the low 50s, and my fingers and toes were starting to feel numb. Wishing I had warm gloves, boots, or a ticket to the Virgin Islands, we kept riding.

A break from the rain in Hornillos del Camino

Soon we arrived at a site of what looked like the ruins of an old church. A tall arch rose over the Camino, and we found shelter underneath it from the rain.

These were the remains of the ancient monastery of San Antón, run by the Order of Hospitallers of St. Anthony in the Middle Ages. These monks cared for pilgrims afflicted with "St. Anthony's Fire," a horrific disease caused by a parasitic fungus that came from eating moldy rye bread. Once you hear how bad it was, I guarantee you'll take a closer look the next time you order a Reuben.

The infected person would initially appear crazy, often dancing a jig known as the "St. Anthony dance." If left untreated, blood flow to the extremities became restricted, creating a burning sensation, hence the "Fire." Dancing was obviously less enjoyable at this stage.

Next, gangrene set in, causing the fingers and toes—and even hands and feet—to fall off. Perhaps the only upside here was that, now rid of one's extremities, the fiery feeling went away. Then, as if things couldn't get any worse, hallucinations, insomnia, body sores, and convulsions kicked in. The disease affected millions of people and killed hundreds of thousands in the Middle Ages.

The Order of Hospitallers was established in 1100 to help care for those with the sickness, and by 1500, they ran nearly 400 hospitals all over Europe. Some people with the "Fire" would walk the Camino in hopes of being cured. Miraculously, it often worked.

Was it really a miracle? Or something else? In those days, bread was a big part of the diet. The monastery and albergue hosts along the Camino would typically serve wheat bread to pilgrims at dinner, not rye bread which was the staple in other areas of Europe. After a month off the rye, sick pilgrims were arriving in Santiago in much better health.

Without the benefit of clinical trials, placebos, research

labs, or big data, some people started making the connection. By 1600, word was spreading throughout Europe that rye was the culprit. Soon, everyone was switching to wheat. After over 500 years of battling the disease, the problem was solved.

Marty and I walked around the San Antón ruins in the cold rain. I have poor circulation (a condition called Raynaud's), and while my extremities had, in fact, gone numb, I felt relatively confident I was not yet in danger of losing them.

The monastery originally straddled the Camino path, and the arch under which we were standing was originally a tunnel where the brothers would receive sick pilgrims. We saw several walls which were the sides of the original church, with openings that once held stained glass windows. A crucifix hung on one side—part of the original altar sanctuary. The whole place had a post-apocalyptic feel.

San Antón

We resumed riding in the downpour. After another hour, now 25 miles into the day, I was chilled to my core and desperately needed to get out of the rain. Just then, we spotted a castle on a hill and a small village below—it was Castrojeriz. We were optimistic we would find a place there to eat and warm up.

Castrojeriz is a small village near the confluence of the Odra and Pisuerga Rivers. Like other Camino towns, the Celts were here first, followed by the Romans, the Visigoths, and then the Spanish. Each built fortresses atop the hill. At an altitude of nearly 3,000 feet, the summit commands a view of the entire surrounding area, which enabled its inhabitants to see the enemy coming from miles away. Late in the ninth century, the Moors made an attempt to attack the castle, but it was successfully defended by Count Muño of Castile. The village has several churches as well as the Convento de Santa Clara, still inhabited by the Poor Clares, an order of nuns founded by St. Clare of Assisi.

Castrojeriz

Looking around, we saw a small eatery with picnic tables outside. We were completely soaked, so we got under an overhang and began digging through our packs, looking for dry clothes. I pulled out several Ziploc bags and located two dry bike shirts, a pair of shorts, and some socks. The only long-sleeved jersey I'd brought was wet from the morning's ride, so I would need to ward off the cold in the afternoon by wearing two short-sleeved shirts.

Still shivering, with dry clothes in hand, we went inside. A welcome blast of warm air greeted us as we entered. It was a small, cozy place that resembled an Irish pub. A bar ran the length of the room in the back, and a dozen tables were placed on the wood floor in the main area. Nearly every seat was taken with other pilgrims thawing out.

Marty and I took turns changing in the tiny bathroom. I went first. I peeled off the water-logged gear and used a small towel to dry my body. My fingers and toes looked like white prunes and had lost all feeling. After a few minutes, I warmed up, and the circulation and sensation returned.

I put the clean clothes and socks on, then looked down at my shoes. They were completely soaked. I knew if I put them back on, my socks and feet would be wet within seconds.

Looking around, I spotted the empty Ziploc bags that had contained my dry clothes. Why not give them a try? I put two Ziplocs over my dry socks, then slipped on the wet shoes. I looked completely idiotic, but it worked.

Feeling somewhat human again, I went up to the bar.

"Menu, por favor?" I asked.

"This is a bar, we don't serve food," said the bartender flatly, in English.

"No food?" I looked around and saw others eating. "But..."

"Just pizza and paella."

I was curious why pizza and paella didn't count as food, but I didn't press it. Besides, it made our decision easy.

"One of each, please. And hot coffee."

Marty plowed down a whole pizza while I devoured the paella. As we ate, we chatted with some pilgrims. We met two men from Ireland who said they'd seen some astonishing things in the rain that morning. One woman was pushing a child in a stroller along the entire Camino. Another woman in a wheelchair was propelling herself, except on the rocky or bumpy sections where her two sons would help her.

We spoke with Jean and Nathalie, a couple who had biked all the way from their home in Belgium and, like us, had begun their day in Burgos. They were in good spirits and didn't seem nearly as soggy and spent as we were.

"Are you riding the Camino path or the road?" Marty asked.

"Some of each," replied Jean.

"Same with us," I said. "How do you know which to ride when? I've been using Google Maps on my phone, but that only seems to work once we've already decided to get off the Camino onto the road."

"Here, look," said Jean.

Jean showed us the small Garmin devices attached to their handlebars. They had downloaded GPS tracks for their entire trip from a Belgian cycling website and were using them to navigate. These were tried-and-true routes that had been vetted by hundreds of cyclists. They eliminated the guesswork of when they should be on the Camino and when they should take the road.

They also showed us their rain gear—fully waterproof shells, pants and gloves, as well as booties to cover their riding shoes. We suddenly felt very underprepared.

"How far are you riding today?" Marty asked.

"That was enough for us for today. We're stopping here," said Jean. "How about you?"

"Carrión de los Condes," I said.

Jean did some quick mental math and raised his eyebrows. It was 30 miles away, and it was already nearly 2:00 p.m.

"It is quite far, no?"

"Yes," I admitted, hanging my head.

"Bon chance!" he said.

We said goodbye to the cyclists, then pulled out our passports to get them stamped. Mine was wet, but I had the bartender stamp it anyway and made a mental note that I'd need to set it out to dry that night.

Now mostly dry and warm and our stomachs full, we stepped outside. The sky was clearing, and the sun was actually coming out. Things were looking up.

Warm and dry after pizza and paella lunch in Castrojeriz

22

NECESITO AYUDA

CASTROJERIZ TO CARRIÓN DE LOS CONDES

Our spirits buoyed by the sunshine, we returned to the Camino. The morning's rain had left behind a minefield of puddles, and the trail was very muddy. After a half-mile, Marty and I stopped to assess the situation.

"Jumbo, we need to take it very slowly here to avoid splashing the pilgrims."

"Yeah, I agree. But we've got thirty miles to go—this is gonna take forever. By the way, how's your rack?"

"Hanging in there. But thirty more miles of this could start to shake things loose again. How about we take the road this afternoon?"

I got out my phone, brought up Google Maps, and found a road route that would take us to Carrión de los Condes. Unfortunately, it veered away from the Camino to the north, adding more miles, but we felt the smoother ride would be worth the added distance. We backtracked a bit, found the pavement, and began our ride for the afternoon.

We navigated several roundabouts, then followed a two-lane road with a narrow shoulder which undulated through an area of wheat fields. Each time a car whizzed by, it rattled my nerves.

After about an hour, the road crossed over a canal, and we spotted a towpath alongside it that looked rideable. A quick consultation with Google confirmed that the towpath would take us in the general direction of Carrión de los Condes and would enable us to get off the road. We decided to take it.

This was the Canal de Castilla, which runs for 130 miles through northern Spain. They started building it in 1753, with the goal of enabling wheat trade between Castile and other nearby regions. It took nearly a century to complete and was ultimately used for only twenty years, between 1850 and 1870. During this time, 400 barges were towed up and down the canal by mules and oxen. Like the canals in the U.S., by the late 1800s, the railroads in Spain had rendered it obsolete. Today, certain sections are used for irrigating crops, including the portion we had just discovered.

Canal de Castilla

Marty and I left the road and joined the towpath. It immediately brought back fond memories of our rides on the C&O Canal from Cumberland, MD to Washington, DC.

Just as we were settling into a peaceful ride along the left side of the canal, Google indicated we should "turn right."

Turn right? I looked at my screen. Indeed, it wanted us to cross the canal and take a dirt path on the other side through the wheat fields.

We were stumped. We looked around—there was no bridge or any way to get across. And the water was clearly too deep to ride or wade through. We were the only people on the towpath, so there was no one to ask.

"Let's backtrack a bit," Marty suggested. "I think I saw a path branching off not far behind us."

We rode back about 50 yards. Sure enough, we found another trail which intersected the towpath and curved toward the canal. We followed it downhill and through a tunnel—*underneath* the canal.

This was an aqueduct—a water bridge—probably built to allow livestock and people to get from one side of the canal to the other in the 1800s. *How did Google know about it?*

Having successfully "turned right," we continued pedaling on the dirt path as it led away from the canal and into a farm, passing one sunflower field after another. At this point, we hadn't seen anyone for over an hour. Knowing we were far from the Camino—and any sign of civilization—I was becoming concerned. And I was getting tired.

As the afternoon wore on, a headwind began to develop. It started out as a breeze but soon kicked up to about fifteen miles per hour. The treeless landscape allowed the wind to travel unchecked until it reached us, our bodies and panniers catching the air like sails on a boat. I quickly realized that a fully loaded bike and a headwind are a bad combination. Add some mud and a few puddles, and you have a recipe for very slow riding. Despite pedaling hard, we were moving at only two or three miles per hour.

The morning's cold rain had already taken a toll on me. My

back was angry. My legs had formed a union and were threatening to go on strike. My bike seat and butt wanted a divorce.

"This headwind is a mental game, Jumbo. It plays with your mind. Don't let it win. Just keep pedaling."

Google led us through a barren area along a primitive dirt-and-grass path, likely used by an occasional four-wheel drive farming vehicle. But our vehicles were one-wheel drive, and we were probably the first cyclists to ever traverse this stretch. We passed two cows who stared silently back at us. I could read their minds: *These guys are insane. Must be the early stages of St. Anthony's Fire.*

At around 4:00 p.m., as we climbed a hill, the wind became even stronger and I had to walk my bike. At the top, I got back in the saddle, relieved at the thought of coasting down the other side. Just as I began the descent, a gust blew me to a dead stop. I had to pedal hard to get *down* the hill. So much for coasting.

At the bottom, the trail leveled out again. Each stroke was a struggle, but I kept cranking. Then, suddenly, I stopped moving altogether. This time it wasn't the wind. It felt like something was grabbing at my rear wheel.

What was happening? I looked below me—my wheels were sinking into the mud. I tried hard to pedal, but my rear wheel kept spinning and sinking deeper.

Quicksand? I thought. *Marty, get your water bottle ready. My ashes are coming your way.* I looked behind me—Marty was spinning and sinking too.

"Clay!" yelled Marty.

"What do we do?!" I yelled back. I was panicking.

"Stop pedaling! Get off the bike!"

We managed to pull our bikes out of the muck and off to the side of the path. Clay was everywhere—in our chains, the brakes, and the gears. The brown goo had completely filled the gap between my front tire and fork, keeping the front wheel from spinning. And a half-inch layer of the stuff had completely encased our tires. Now we knew where the raw material came from that fed the clay tile ovens in Hornillos centuries ago.

Marty took one of his bottles and squirted water onto his bike. After depleting half of the precious liquid, he realized it was no use—the clay was stuck to everything like glue.

I assumed we were done. We'd need to abandon the bikes, sling our packs over our shoulders, and walk. We had nearly 20 miles to go—it would take us all night. Between us, we had twelve ounces of water and ten Peanut M&Ms. We might have to resort to cannibalism. Perhaps some shepherd would find our decomposed bodies out here 800 years from now. Would they build a shrine? Would people make pilgrimages? Probably not.

"Jumbo, here, try this."

Marty had pulled a screwdriver from his bag and was using it to pry the clay loose. It was painstaking, but it seemed to be working.

He handed me the screwdriver, and I did the same. Once I'd freed my front wheel from its frozen state, I tried to ride the bike to see if spinning the wheels would shed some of the clay. Mud will eventually work its way loose when you ride, but the clay held its grip. The bike let out screeching and gnashing sounds, like raccoons fighting in the middle of the night. I stopped, then spent another half-hour cleaning the wheels, brakes, chain and sprockets.

We then pushed our bikes in the grass alongside the path for a few hundred yards. The condition of the path improved a little, becoming more solid and rocky, so we started riding again. We could still hear our brakes grinding as we moved. And the headwind hadn't given up.

All of a sudden, I felt a jerking tug on my rear wheel. I stopped and looked back. My rack and panniers had come loose and were dangling over to the left side, causing the rack to rub against my back tire. Marty's rack had been causing intermittent problems throughout the whole trip, but until now, mine had been indestructible. *What was going on?*

There was so much clay in and around my rack that I couldn't identify the problem. But it was obvious that my bike was not rideable. I showed Marty, and we both agreed to dismount. I removed my packs, slung them over my shoulders, and began walking my bike.

We trudged along the path, the sun beating down on us, the unrelenting wind in our faces, and the straps on my saddlebags digging into my shoulders.

Then, just when things couldn't get worse, they got worse.

In front of us was an enormous puddle—more accurately, a pond—that spanned the entire path. We tried to find a way around it, but tall, thick grass hugged the trail on both sides.

"Jumbo, looks like we gotta go through it."

Marty went first. He tried riding, but the water was so deep and the muck so thick that he had to dismount. He walked through the rest of the puddle, the water up to his knees.

I paused at the water's edge to muster up my courage. My feet had been in the Ziploc bags since lunchtime, and by now my shoes had started to dry. That wasn't going to last.

I stepped into the pond with my bike beside me. Several steps later, I was up to my knees. A cold, wet sensation enveloped my feet as the water breached the Ziplocs.

I looked down at the brown water. *There could be anything in here—snakes, leeches, piranhas...* I gritted my teeth and kept moving. Looking ahead, I saw Marty exiting the lake. Thankfully it hadn't gotten much deeper. I pressed on and soon joined him on the other side.

We took stock—our shoes were sopping wet and covered with mud, as were our legs from the knees down. With no other option, we kept walking.

By 6:30 p.m., we had covered 55 miles, the total distance we'd originally planned for the day. However, in getting off the Camino, we had taken a much longer route and still had ten miles to go. At this pace, we would arrive at Carrión de los Condes well after dark. We were all alone, on a remote farming path, far from the Camino.

People react differently to adverse situations. I get quiet. I stop talking. I lose my sense of humor. I start to imagine worst-case scenarios. I let my mind play out those scenarios. My emotions begin to take over. I get frustrated. And then I start to panic.

I left my comfortable home and bed in Pittsburgh—for this? I'm sixty years old. I'm a grandfather, for God's sake. This would be stupid even for a 20-year-old. No one forced me to do this. I'm doing it voluntarily. I'm actually spending money to do it! It took months to plan this trip. It was supposed to be fun. What the hell am I doing out here?

I was physically and mentally exhausted. I was starting to feel desperate and said a prayer. Actually, I screamed it.

"Jumbo, easy man. Sit down, take a break."

Marty had no idea where we were, what time it was, where we were staying, or how far we had to go. In his blissfully ignorant state, he wasn't at all worried about being stranded on the Camino at night. But he *was* worried about something—me.

"I'd really like to rest, Marty, but we can't stop. We're gonna be stuck out here in the dark."

"Jumbo, we'll be okay. Take a deep breath. It'll all be fine. Pinch yourself—we're in Spain!"

How could he be so relaxed? We're in big trouble—can't he see that? This is a disaster. We're not gonna make it.

We plodded along, my back throbbing under the weight of the saddlebags. I wanted it to end.

Just then, I spotted something in the distance. It looked like a small one-story building. Was it a mirage? Was I hallucinating? As we got closer, it came into view.

It was a gas station. In the middle of nowhere, a gas station.

I once watched a documentary about a ship that sunk in the middle of the ocean. Several dozen men were left floating on lifeboats and rafts—exposed to the sun, fending off sharks, and deprived of food for weeks. When they finally saw land in the distance, some became so hysterical that they dove into the water and started swimming toward the far-off shore.

I'm not saying this was like that. But I'm also not saying it wasn't. That gas station was going to save us. I felt like either jumping for joy or passing out. Actually, both.

A few minutes later, we arrived at the station. The place looked empty, except for a van parked beside one of the pumps. A man was standing next to it, filling up his tank.

As we approached, we nodded to him, and he nodded back. We found a bench and sat down, trying to determine what to do next. I was fixated on the van.

"Marty, I'm gonna ask him if he can give us a ride."

"Whoa, Jumbo, first let's figure out what we wanna do here."

The man finished filling his car, replaced the nozzle, and paid with his credit card.

"I'm done, Marty. I can't ride any more. If we wait, he'll be gone. It'll be dark in an hour. This guy could be our only chance. I'm gonna try."

I walked over to him, my entire body covered in clay and mud. He spoke no English, so I used one of the few Spanish phrases I'd learned before the trip.

"Uhh... *necesito ayuda—bicicleta.*" (I need help—bicycle). I pointed to my broken bike.

It didn't take much for him to understand our predicament. "*Sí!*" he said. Immediately, he opened up the back of his van. "*Ponla aquí!*" (Put it here!)

The van was pristinely clean inside. It actually looked brand new. I pointed at the dirt on our bikes.

"Are you sure?" I asked.

Without hesitating, he grabbed my bike and loaded it in the back, the mud smearing all over his clean carpeting. He then motioned to Marty, who followed suit and lifted his bike into the van.

"Carrión de los Condes?" In my panicked state, I had neglected to tell him where we were going. And he hadn't even asked. It must have been obvious how distressed we were.

"*Sí, no pasa nada.*" (No problem.)

I sat next to him in the front seat, trying in vain to avoid soiling the upholstery. Marty took the back seat. He pulled out of the station and onto the road. I tried to communicate, but it was no use, so we sat there in silence as we watched the landscape roll by. A feeling of relief began to wash over me.

After about ten minutes, we saw a sign for Carrión de los Condes. He pulled into a parking lot just off the road.

"*Un kilómetro,*" he said, raising his index finger. We gathered that he wasn't able to drive us all the way to our hotel, but we didn't have too far to go.

We got out of the van, and he helped us pull out our bikes. I tried to hand him twenty euros to thank him. He shook his head. "Please, take it," I said. He politely refused the money, shook our hands with a smile and a "gracias," and drove away.

Camino Angel #3.

23

THE ENGLISH MENU
CARRIÓN DE LOS CONDES

I t was dark. We limped our bikes into Carrión de Los Condes, my panniers strapped over my shoulders, bumping my rib cage with each step. Using our cell phone flashlights, we eventually found our hotel. The owner, Julia, met us there.

"I was worried about you!" *She wasn't the only one.* "Look at you both, you're a mess! Are you okay?"

"Yes, pretty tired but we're okay," said Marty.

She took us down to the garage where we parked our cycles. Then she led us up to the apartment, showed us around, and took extra time to make up the sofa bed for me.

"If you need any help with your bikes tomorrow, here's the name and number of a local mechanic," she said. "Oh, and here's a restaurant where you can go tonight. It's the only place in town open this late." She handed me a piece of paper.

"Thank you so much."

"If you need anything else, just call me," she said as she headed out the door.

Next came the task of washing our clothes. I took off my damp, muddy shoes, removed the Ziploc bags, and pulled off my socks, which were saturated from the stroll through the pond. We had gone through two full sets of clothes—virtually everything we'd brought was filthy and wet. I opened the bag with the shirt and shorts I'd worn in the morning and dumped them out. They landed on the floor with a thud, along with a few clumps of meseta.

Marty did the same, and I threw everything into the washer.

"Hungry?" Marty asked.

"Starving."

In the darkness, Marty and I walked to the center of town, found the restaurant Julia had recommended, and stepped inside. We were the only patrons there, and they were starting to close up. Nevertheless, the waitress led us to a table with a smile. We sat down and started looking at our menus. Everything was in Spanish.

"English?" Marty asked the waitress.

"Sí," she replied. She went behind the counter and returned with a piece of graph paper with handwriting on it. I handed Marty my reading glasses.

"Jumbo, this first course, 'Rice with Seafood (Fish)'—I guess the 'Fish' is to help us Americans know what 'seafood' is?" Marty was chuckling, trying to cheer me up.

I responded matter-of-factly. "I think it's to let you know you're not getting scallops or shrimp or something. Just fish."

Marty kept studying the page, getting a kick out of the handwritten translations. "Look down there at the second course—'Sea Bass *Fish*.' Glad they clarified that. There's also the lesser-known 'Sea Bass *Pork*', you know. Oh, and check out the 'Grilled Loin.' I guess that gives them options, right? They can serve you whatever they happen to have—beef, pork, lamb..."

I forced a laugh, but was having a hard time re-gaining my sense of humor after the grueling day. We ordered some food and a couple of beers. Marty could tell I was beat.

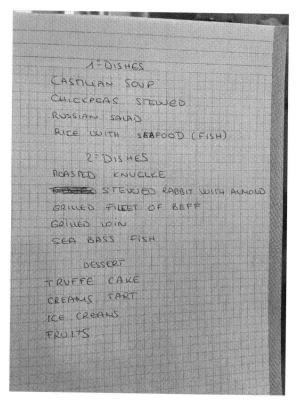

English menu in Carrión de los Condes

"Jumbo, are you okay?"

"Not really," I said. "That was the hardest day of my life."

"Yeah, it was a beast alright." Five years older than me, Marty looked like he could have ridden another ten miles.

"The rain, the cold, the wind, the clay—plus not knowing where we're going—is making it really tough. My back is hurting, and my rack is broken. I'm too old for this, Marty."

Marty looked at me and thought for a few moments.

"You're not too old for this, Jumbo. But how about we take tomorrow off? Take a bus to the next town. Give you a chance to rest and fix your bike before tackling the second half."

I felt bad that I was slowing Marty down. But I knew there was no way I could ride 60 miles to León the next day.

"Yeah, I think that's a good idea," I agreed.

"Jumbo, it's gonna be fine. This has got to be fun. It's no good if you're not having fun." Then he stood up, walked over to me, and gave me a big bear hug. "I need my Jumbo back."

"Thanks man."

Relieved at the thought of resting the next day, I enjoyed the meal. And the beer went exactly where it needed to go.

We headed back to our hotel. As we opened the door to our room, we saw Julia in the hallway.

"Buenas noches! How was dinner?"

"Great, thank you for the recommendation," I said.

"Were you able to use the washing machine?"

"Yes, no problem."

"I'm sorry there's no dryer. I can help with the drying rack."

"Thanks, but I think we can figure it..."

Before I could finish, Julia was already walking into our room. We watched as she pulled out a drying rack, set it up, and unloaded our clothes from the washer. She then proceeded to carefully lay everything out, socks and underwear included. As a final measure, she set up a fan and pointed it at the rack to help the clothes dry faster. It took her over half an hour.

"Muchas gracias," said Marty.

"De nada," she said. "Sleep well!" Camino Angel #4.

I sat down and nearly fell asleep in the chair. But we had one more thing to do before crashing—find a bus the next day to León. I got on my phone and located the website of a bus company which ran the route we were looking for. I bought two tickets using my credit card.

"Done, Marty, I got the tickets. The bus leaves at ten a.m. That'll actually give us more time to see León once we get there. Let's get some sleep."

The trip is in charge.

24

COME MONDAY
CARRIÓN DE LOS CONDES

I opened my eyes. For a moment, I thought the previous day's ride had been a bad dream. Did it actually happen? As I pulled myself out of the sofa bed, the aches in my thighs, rear end, and lower back were an immediate reminder that it was no dream. I was hurting.

We got dressed, packed up our panniers, and went back to the garage. Our bikes looked like they had been through a minor land war. My rack was still dangling off the side of the rear wheel. Mud and clay were everywhere—in the chain and cassette, on the wheels and tires, and all over the frame. I bought a kitchen brush from a convenience store next to our hotel. We squirted water from our bottles and scrubbed... and scrubbed some more.

Once we had gotten our bikes to the point where they were once again recognizable as bicycles, I inspected my rack. I was pleasantly surprised to see that it was not actually broken. One of the screws attaching it to the hub area had come loose and disappeared, lost somewhere in the meseta. Marty removed a screw from his second bottle cage and offered to let me use it to secure my rack. It worked.

As I was attaching my packs to my newly rehabilitated rack, I realized I had lost something else the previous day. My scallop shell, that ever-present totem which had been jiggling on the side of my bag since leaving Pamplona, was gone. That shell had started life somewhere in the ocean, made its way to a Pittsburgh raw bar, then to Spain, only to be buried in the mud in the meseta. I mourned briefly, then thought perhaps a stray pilgrim would find it someday and bring it to Santiago so it could complete its pilgrimage.

We rode slowly through town to the bus station. When we arrived around 9:30 a.m., we saw it was not actually a station—it was a tiny bus stop. I examined the schedule posted on the side. It showed a 10:00 a.m. departure to León every day except Mondays. I checked our tickets. They were for Tuesday at 10:00 a.m.—I was glad to see they matched the posted schedule. We leaned our bikes against the shelter and began to relax. The bus should arrive in 30 minutes.

Just then, a panic hit me.

"Marty, what day is today?"

"You're asking *me* what day it is?" he chortled.

"Seriously, what day is it? It's Tuesday, right?"

Still cackling, Marty got out his phone and tapped on it. "It's Monday, Jumbo."

"Ahhh... damn it!" I screamed. "I screwed up! I bought the tickets for the wrong day. Look, the bus doesn't even run today."

"Jumbo, that's great!" Marty was smiling and looking strangely upbeat.

"What's great about it?! There's *nothing* great about it!"

"You've officially lost track of days!" Marty was beaming. "It means you're really starting to chill. I love it!"

I couldn't help but shake my head and laugh along with him. The trip is in charge.

"What now, Marty?"

"Remember? No major decisions without espresso."

We spotted a café—Bar España—just across from the bus stop. We walked our bikes over to it. It was a busy place, with many pilgrims fueling up for the day's hike.

Seated outside with our coffee and pastries, we discussed our situation. We didn't want to wait until the next day, so we decided a taxi would be our next best option. We would need one big enough to hold two bikes, and it would likely not be cheap as it was over an hour's drive to León.

While we were sipping our coffee, we saw a large taxi-van drive up. It picked up two pilgrims and drove away. It seemed we weren't the only ones taking a day off.

I asked our waitress about the taxi. She said that the café's owner, Mariano, was also a taxi driver. We asked whether he would take us to León. She said after he finished driving the passengers we'd just seen leaving, he would return and take us at noon. That gave us a little time to see the town, so we paid our bill, got a passport stamp, and walked around.

Situated on the river Carrión, Carrión de los Condes was a Moorish stronghold until the late 700s. Around that time, a Knight named Alonso Carreño defeated the Moors here, took over the village, and for some reason decided to celebrate by changing his name to "Carrión." The town was named after him: Carrión de los Condes means "Carrión of the Counts."

The village had a large population of Jewish people in the 12th through 14th centuries who were often persecuted by the Christian minority. One day, a large group of Carrión's Christians killed two Jewish citizens. The king responded by hanging ten of the Christian ringleaders and throwing the rest in prison. However, this didn't stop the persecution—eventually most of the Jews relented and became baptized as Christians.

Marty and I checked out the town's two 12th century churches—the Iglesia de Santa María de las Victorias and the Iglesia de Santiago. The latter houses a famous sculpted frieze above the doorway called the Pantocrator, a masterpiece of Romanesque art.

Iglesia de Santa Maria de las Victorias, Carrión de los Condes

We returned to the café, and within a few minutes our taxi pulled up. We took off our front wheels and helped Mariano load the bikes inside. Marty and I jumped in the back seat as he steered the van out of town and into the meseta toward León.

25

THE COLONOSCOPY
CARRIÓN DE LOS CONDES TO LEÓN

Sunflowers on the meseta

We tried communicating with Mariano during the taxi ride, but it was no use as he spoke no English. On the highway, looking out the window at the vast sunflower fields, Marty broke the silence.

"Hey Jumbo, you had your colonoscopy a couple of weeks ago, right? Just before the trip?"

Colonoscopy? Where was this coming from?

"Yup, I did." I played along, hoping Mariano wouldn't be able to follow the conversation, wherever it might be headed.

"How'd it go?" Marty asked.

"It went fine."

"Just *fine*?"

"Yeah, all good. He told me I didn't have any polyps or anything."

"So the doctor really didn't say anything else?" Marty was chuckling. Now I knew exactly where he was going with this. But a little background is helpful here.

As explained earlier, since Marty is three years older than Belle and five years older than Katie and me, we have an understanding that Marty will be the "first to go" (i.e., check out, kick the bucket, push up daisies). Naturally, this means that as long as Marty is above ground, we can go on living our happy lives.

With this in mind, when Marty turned 50, all three of us encouraged him to get his first colonoscopy. He didn't want to do it and kept putting it off. Several years later, he finally gave in.

Marty completed the prep the night before, which he oddly said he enjoyed. Why?

"I liked the feeling of having everything cleaned out in there."

He underwent the procedure, and after the anesthesia wore off, the doctor sat down next to Marty, with Belle by his side.

"How's it look, doc?" Marty asked.

"Well, everything looks very good."

"Anything else you can tell me?"

"Yes, good news—no polyps or anything to be concerned about."

"That's good to hear. Nothing else? No other details?"

The doctor took off his glasses and leaned toward Marty.

"Sir, your colon is extremely clean. In fact, if you had to—not that you'd want to—you could eat off it."

Marty's face broke into a huge smile. He nodded and looked at Belle. Belle rolled her eyes and patted Marty's hand.

"Thanks, doc. I hope I'm never in a situation where I need to do that, but if I do, that's good to know."

A few days later, I was over at Marty's house, and he told me the story.

"There's no way he actually said that, Marty." He had to be making this up.

"That's exactly what he said. Ask Belle. I gotta admit, Jumbo, it sounded a little odd—coming from a doctor—but I guess it's a good thing."

"What kind of situation would cause one to *have* to eat off a colon?" I asked. I couldn't believe I was actually engaging in this.

"Well, I suppose if someone were to put a gun to your head and say 'eat off that colon,' you'd have to do it, right?" Marty posited.

"Yeah, clearly that would be one of those cases."

"Or, if you were having a picnic, and you forgot to bring a tablecloth or paper plates..."

"True," I nodded.

"I'm not sure how that would actually work," said Marty.

"What?"

"Eating off a colon. Like... how do you actually *do* that? I just can't picture it."

"Let's just hope none of us ever has to do it."

❧

Back to the discussion during the taxi ride across the meseta about my recent colonoscopy, which I told Marty "went fine."

"So the doctor really didn't say anything else? Nothing else?" Marty wanted desperately for me to take the bait as we droned along.

I rolled my eyes. "No, Marty, he didn't say I could eat off it."

"No? Did you ask him?"

"I don't think that's something you ask your doctor. I think they either offer it or they don't," I said.

"Well, if it were really, really clean, I have to believe he would have said it." Marty was clearly gloating about his immaculate digestive tract.

"So, you think it's part of the standard bedside manner rubric they're taught in medical school? About how to deliver colonoscopy results to patients?" I asked.

"I do," said Marty confidently. "I'm guessing they're given a bar chart. At the bottom, it's red—that's where they have to deliver the bad news. You know, like 'I'm sorry sir, you may need surgery and treatment...' In the middle section, it's yellow, basically meaning 'you have some polyps, we need to keep an eye on them.'"

"I get it, so at the top, it's green—that's essentially what I got. 'You're good, all clear, come back in ten years.'"

"Right," Marty nodded. "And then at the *very* top, there's a teeny, tiny 'green plus' area with a small fork and knife icon on the side. And under that it says, 'Instruct the patient they can eat off it, if needed.'"

I was howling. "How big is that area, do you think?"

"I'll bet it's a tiny sliver. Like... less than one percent. I have a top one percent colon, Jumbo," Marty said proudly.

"In fact," he continued, "I actually have some data on this. I took Belle in for *her* colonoscopy a few months ago. Afterwards, in the recovery room, I sat next to her bed as she was coming off the anesthesia. While I was waiting, I watched the doctor making his way around the room, talking to half a dozen other patients as they woke up. Not once did I overhear the phrase 'eat off it.'"

"And when Belle woke up? What did he tell her?"

"He said it looked 'fine.' No issues."

"So she's probably in the green on that bar chart, right?"

"Right, but no fork and knife," Marty waved his finger. "I'm the only one I know of who has reached that level."

I shook my head and laughed as I looked out the window at the landscape whizzing by. I let Marty enjoy this moment. There are hundreds of ways Marty could go (first), but at least we had ruled out one of them.

26

OF BLISTERS AND PASTRIES

LEÓN

Mariano stopped the taxi just outside León's center and helped Marty and me unload our bikes. We mounted them and rode slowly into town.

León was busy—it was the third largest city we'd visited, with a population of around 125,000. To use a now-familiar refrain (sing it with me), it was originally inhabited by the Celts, settled by the Romans, sacked by the Visigoths, and taken by Moors in the eighth century.

In the ninth century, the city was reclaimed by Spain during the Reconquest and became the capital of the Kingdom of León. This began a time of prosperity and influence for León that lasted four centuries. But by the 13th century, the nearby Kingdom of Castile had ascended in power, and Castile annexed León to its crown. This caused the city to decline in prominence, and a 600-year period of stagnation followed.

Then, in the 19th and 20th centuries, León's economy and population staged a comeback, thanks to coal mining and the arrival of the railroad. People from nearby rural areas began migrating into the urban center. León is now a beautiful city bustling with tourists, locals, and Camino pilgrims, along with many buildings that serve as reminders of its rich history.

Marty and I checked into our Airbnb and then headed out to walk around. Just outside our apartment stood the 13th century Gothic León Cathedral, commanding an impressive presence on the central Plaza de Regla. We toured the cathedral and marveled at the stained glass, considered one of the most spectacular displays in all of Europe.

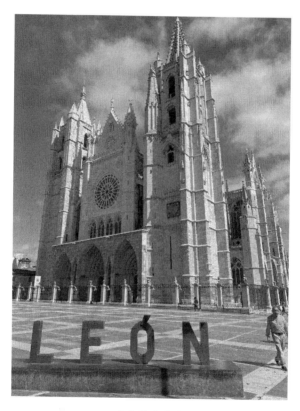

León Cathedral

Next, we saw the Casa Botines, a massive building designed by Antoni Gaudi in the late 1800s as a place of commerce for cloth merchants. Now a museum, its architecture differed completely from everything else we'd seen—sort of "modern medieval." We also saw some well-preserved sections of the Roman walls which once surrounded the entire town.

Casa Botines, designed by Antoni Gaudi

In need of a beer, we found at a café on the Plaza de Regla facing the cathedral. Seated outside at a big table was a group of pilgrims who had become friends while walking the Camino from St. Jean Pied de Port. They invited us to join them.

Jenna, a corporate executive in her early 60s, was rubbing her knee and wincing. She was from the Isle of Man, a small Celtic island in the Irish Sea between England and Ireland (which, evidently, also has some female residents). For Jenna, this was a long-awaited opportunity for an extended break and an adventure. She had used a Camino planning agency to book nice hotels along the way, including one in León. She planned to get back on the Camino the next morning.

The other members of Jenna's "Camino family" were staying in albergues and would rendezvous each morning with her before heading out. They included Hung from Vietnam, Adele from Hamburg, Lily from London, and two cousins from Australia in their twenties—Charlie and Logan. Charlie still lived in Australia, while Logan had moved to the U.K. They get together once a year to do a "walkabout" somewhere in the world. The Camino seemed to fit that bill pretty well.

Most conversations among pilgrims start with a discussion about the status of one's blisters. We found they are often described as being in one of four stages:

"Bubbling"

"Seeping"

"Weeping"

"Bleeding"

After everyone has shared the location and severity of their blisters, they then debate their strategies for treating them. Each pilgrim seems to have a different approach that he or she *swears* is best. Some apply moleskin, some use gauze, some pop them and rip the skin off, and some do nothing. You would think that after a thousand years of feet tramping on the Camino, there would be a generally-accepted way of dealing with these painful vesicles. Or, even better, some method for not getting them in the first place.

As we joined the conversation at the café, the blister discussion was well underway.

Lily's blisters were "weeping" by Carrión de los Condes, yet she'd still powered through two more days of agony on the Camino. At that point, she'd had enough and took a taxi to León. She was planning to head back to London and complete her Camino the next year. However, she wanted to see the group one more time, so she'd waited for them to arrive here before flying home.

"I don't get blisters," said Charlie.

"Really?" I asked.

"I'll tell ya my secret if ya wanna know."

"What is it?"

"I soak my feet in Vaseline, then wear two pairs of socks."

"And then your boots over the socks?" I asked.

"Nope. Just a cheap pair of trainers." He showed us his running shoes. "Boots are too heavy."

"But those shoes aren't waterproof. When it rains, don't your wet feet drive you crazy?" Marty asked.

Charlie quickly answered, "Well, the great thing is that yer feet already feel wet from the Vaseline, so it doesn't really bother ya."

"How 'bout you blokes?" asked Logan.

"No blisters so far. We're biking," said Marty.

"That's cheating!!" interjected Charlie. "That's doing it the easy way!"

"Well, I guess it is in some ways," said Marty. "But this trail was never made for bikes, so to be honest, it's pretty tough."

Most Australians we'd met on the Camino seemed to party very hard and smoke constantly. Charlie and Logan were no exception—both were enjoying a cigarette as we chatted.

"I really need to quit these," said Logan. "But I figure if I walk 800 kilometers, it should cancel out some o' the bad stuff."

We laughed along with them. "What are you all doing tonight?"

"Gonna get piss drunk," said Charlie with a grin. "Got an extra day here in the albergue, so I have time to recover."

Charlie and Logan were taking a rest day in León, a common strategy as León is roughly at the midpoint of the Camino. With the others in the group moving on in the morning, tonight was a night to party hard.

"How well do you sleep in those albergues?" Marty asked.

"With four bottles of wine in ya, ya can sleep anywhere."

At the time, I assumed that meant two for Charlie and two for Logan. But now that I think about it, he probably meant four bottles each. They would need that rest day.

It was mid-afternoon, and Marty and I were famished. Since the restaurants in Spain don't serve dinner until after 7:00 p.m., we stepped inside the café to see what snack offerings they might have. The case below the bar contained mostly pastries. On the far end, we spotted a tray of sliced bread, each with a thin sliver of ham on top.

Marty got the bartender's attention and pointed to the bread/ham combo snacks. "Dos?"

"No," she said, shaking her head. This was becoming a pattern. *Why didn't they want to serve us food in the bars in Spain?*

He shrugged his shoulders. "Why not?"

"Cerveza," she said, pointing at the beer tap.

Through sign and body language, we gathered that we couldn't actually buy the snacks. They provide them for free when you buy a beer—and only if you ask for them. The fact that we'd already bought two beers apparently didn't count. So we bought two more beers and received what we really wanted —food. While we were at it, we asked them to stamp our passports.

During the whole exchange, Marty had been taken in by the pastry case. He eyed a massive rectangular pastry with several Napoleon-like flaky layers, topped with three inches of white cream and a crusty lid. The whole thing stood about five inches tall. There were six of them left, sitting on a tray tucked behind some other pastries.

"What is *that*?" I asked.

"I dunno, but that thing looks good. That's me," said Marty.

"You gonna buy one?"

"Not yet."

"What if they run out?"

"I think it's safe. Look, there are a bunch of them there, and they're kind of hidden. I'll come back."

Still killing time until the restaurants opened, Marty and I walked across town and found another outdoor café in the Plaza del Grano. There were two open tables—one was playing host to a flock of pigeons attacking a half-eaten plate of croquettas, so we took the other one. To our surprise, Jenna,

Charlie, and Logan were seated at the next table. The Aussies had a bottle of wine in front of them and were well on their way toward achieving their goal for the evening. Jenna was carrying a shopping bag. Marty asked her what she'd bought.

"Ibuprofen and a knee brace."

At around 7:00 p.m., we said goodbye to the group and found an outdoor restaurant with a front-row view of the now-illuminated cathedral. Seeing couples dining together at nearby tables reminded us of Katie and Belle. By now, we'd been away from them for nine days, and even though we'd been texting with them and talking every few nights, we were missing them.

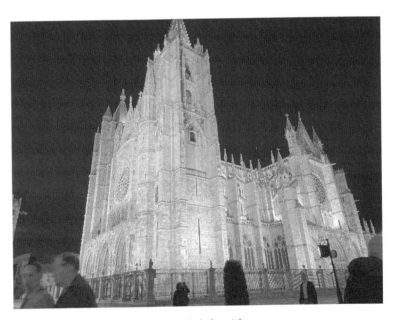

León Cathedral at night

After dinner, we began walking back toward our apartment. But Marty hadn't forgotten about the pastry case.

"Jumbo, let's swing back and buy that thing."

We returned to the café. Looking down at the pastry case,

Marty was horrified to see that it was dark and empty. The entire case had been cleared out. Had they sold everything? Or possibly thrown out the day's leftovers?

Marty got the attention of the woman behind the counter.

"Pastry?" he said, pointing at the vacant case.

She shook her head. "*No entiendo.*" (I don't understand).

Most people would have just let it go at that point. Instead, Marty launched into an Academy Award-winning charades performance as he attempted to describe the pastry for the woman.

"Big," he said, drawing an outline of a large rectangular footprint with his fingers.

She watched him, eyes narrowed, arms folded, head tilted.

"Tall." Marty placed one hand flat on the counter, face up, and held his other hand above it, face down, separated by about ten inches.

"Layers," he said, making repeated sweeping motions with his top hand.

"Cream." He pretended to eat the top layer of the imaginary pastry with an imaginary fork.

"Ahhh! Sí!" she exclaimed. She spun around, went behind the bar, and returned with the tray containing the "thing" Marty had been looking for. There were only two left.

Marty smiled. "Dos? To go?" he asked, holding up two fingers.

It was clearly the first time anyone had ever ordered takeout from this café. She rummaged around, eventually found a paper plate, and pulled out some wax paper. She draped it over the top of the pastries but wasn't happy with the result. So she crumpled up the paper and started over. After trying several times, she finally settled on a satisfactory wrapping strategy and handed the masterpiece to Marty. He paid for them and thanked her.

On the way back to our apartment, a passerby accidentally

bumped Marty's arm. To our shock and horror, the pastries fell onto the cobblestones, wrappings and all. We both stared in disbelief.

"Quick, five seconds!" Marty yelled.

Marty was referring to the "five-second rule," a scientific principle whereby any food dropped on the ground is shielded from dirt, dust, bacteria, and other "debris" for up to five seconds. Any longer than that, all bets are off.

In a rare display of lightning-fast reaction, Marty scrambled to pick up the confections and put them back on the plate. I heard him counting: "One-one-thousand, two-one-thousand..."

They were a complete mess, but based on his swift response, we were confident they were still safe to eat.

Back at our apartment, we plowed into them. Our faces smeared with white cream, we nodded to each other.

"See Jumbo, what'd I tell you? Worth the wait, huh?"

I took a few bites and then stopped.

"Something wrong? Dirt?"

"No, I'm just full."

"Full? What does that have to do with it? This thing is incredible, Jumbo. How can you not eat it all?"

"I'm not hungry."

"Eat it!" Marty laughed.

I took two more bites, then set it aside. "I'm gonna save it for the morning."

"Sheesh. That is some serious willpower."

Marty gobbled his pastry down in less than two minutes. I put the rest of mine in the refrigerator, looking forward to savoring it the next morning with an espresso.

As I got ready for bed, I was bummed that we'd missed riding another stretch of Camino. But I knew it was the right thing to do. My body was feeling better, and my mind was in a better place, too. I'd be ready to get back on the bike tomorrow.

27

MARTY'S BEST FRIEND
LEÓN TO HOSPITAL DE ÓRBIGO

The next morning, as I nibbled on the remains of my pastry, Marty headed back to the café, bought another one, and immediately devoured it. Somehow, my brother-in-law is able to eat vast quantities of junk food, then get on a bike and out-ride anyone. That morning, I dubbed him the "Perfect Pastry Processing Machine."

After a day off, it was time to get back in the saddle. My muscles had more or less recovered from the meseta, and some ice and Advil helped dull the back pain. Marty carried our bikes outside to the courtyard, where he lubricated our chains and attached our panniers. While he worked, dozens of children with backpacks walked past us on their way to school. They were pointing and staring at us, marveling at the sight of two old guys living out an adventure dream.

Well, kids, in another 50 years or so, you can retire and do this too. Just stay focused on your schoolwork for now.

We began our ride from León to Astorga, about 35 miles with 1,500 feet of climbing (Santiago was now 195 miles away). Our first stop was at a bike shop to pump up our tires and get a few things, including more Peanut M&Ms.

On most days, instead of stopping for lunch, we would snack on Peanut M&Ms. In fact, we discovered they are the perfect cycling food. I stored them in the back pocket of my jersey. Even with the heat coming from my body and the sun, their crispy exoskeleton kept them from melting (true to the commercial). They gave us some protein and a sugar boost that lasted all day long.

León was hectic on this Monday morning. We weaved in and out of traffic, trying to avoid getting hit by Spaniards driving to work. Wanting to get off the road, we discovered the Paseo de la Condesa, a long, picturesque esplanade which parallels the Burnesga River. A walking/biking path ran though it, so we left the congestion behind and entered the park.

The path led us past gardens, fountains, and playgrounds to the expansive Plaza de San Marcos. Across the plaza sits the Convento de San Marcos, originally built in the 12th century as a hospital and shelter for Camino pilgrims, now converted to a *parador* (high-end hotel). This is the hotel where Martin Sheen's character (Tom) treats his Camino friends to a luxurious one-night stay as a break from the albergues in "The Way." Marty and I rode around the enormous building but didn't go inside.

Convento de San Marcos

At the edge of the plaza, we spotted a Camino marker which put us on the trail toward Astorga. It was a spectacular 70-degree sunny day. The Camino surface was dry, crushed gravel and packed dirt—we immediately appreciated the absence of clay and standing water. We were at the western edge of the meseta—the gently rolling hills made for easy riding, and the landscape was dotted with farms and an occasional patch of trees. Now *this* is the kind of day you want to be on a bike.

After a few miles, we passed through San Martin del Camino ("St. Marty of the Camino"), an enclave of only 350 residents. San Martin was the Bishop of Tours, France, in the fourth century. He is revered as a patron saint of France and is memorialized in many places along the French Way of the Camino. Given that we'd seen my patron saint literally everywhere for the last week, Marty was happy to see his own saint make an appearance.

Just past San Martin, we noticed a tall terra cotta water tower with what looked like a pile of dead grass on top. As we got closer, we could see it was a massive bird's nest. We talked to some pilgrims who were taking a picture; they told us it was a nesting place for white storks. With a wing span of six to seven feet, these huge birds are common in this area. They build their nests atop churches, in bell towers, and on other tall structures.

While looking at the nest, it occurred to me that—despite spending most of our waking hours outdoors—we hadn't yet seen any wildlife on this trip. This was quite different from our rides in the woods of Pennsylvania, Maryland, and West Virginia, where we'd often see deer, groundhogs, herons, egrets, hawks, turtles, snakes, and even an occasional bear or bald eagle. In Spain, aside from several cows and a few hundred thousand mosquitoes, wildlife had been scarce.

We waited for a few minutes to see if one of the storks would return. Unfortunately, they must have been out on a baby-delivery run. We hopped on our bikes and continued on our way.

Our next stop was the small medieval village of Hospital de Órbigo, on the Órbigo River. Just before the town, Marty and I rode across a long stone bridge with twenty arches spanning the river as well as a large expanse of dry ground below.

"Jousting Bridge" over Órbigo River

Legend has it that Don Suero de Quiñones, a medieval knight on whom "Don Quixote" is based, held a jousting tournament on the bridge in 1434 to earn the favor of a woman who had been ignoring him. Each year, the town celebrates the legend by holding a jousting tournament in June.

"What did you do to earn Belle's favor?" I asked Marty. "Anything dangerous?"

"I don't remember, but I know there wasn't any jousting involved," said Marty, chuckling. "I think I mostly sat around and drank beer until she got interested in me."

"That gets them every time. You're a real Casanova."

At the end of the bridge, Marty and I met three pilgrims—Chris from Maui, Mark from Savannah, and Roxanne from Argentina. Chris was in the tourism industry, and since his business had essentially shut down due to the 2023 Lahaina fires, he figured this was a good time to leave and do something else. Mark was recently retired and had always wanted to travel the Camino. He was holding a walking stick with one hand and rubbing his ankle with the other.

"How has your Camino been?" Marty asked.

"Amazing," said Chris.

"Have you all been together the whole time?"

"I started in St. Jean. So did Mark—we met on the first day, climbing the Napoleon Pass in the Pyrenees."

"How was that?" I asked. "We started in Pamplona so we missed that section."

"By far the hardest day," said Mark. "Walked twenty miles uphill that day. In some places it was really steep. I strained my achilles and Chris helped me get up to the top. Been limping ever since."

So far, Roxanne had been quiet. I looked at her. "How about you?"

"I met them in Pamplona," she said in perfect English. "We've all been traveling together since then."

"It's been over two weeks now—we've become pretty close," said Chris. "Roxanne here is our interpreter. How are you guys making out with the language?"

I smiled and looked at Marty. "Well, Marty is pretty much fluent. He adds an "o" to the ends of English words. Seems to work really well."

They all seemed amused, especially Roxanne. We chatted for a few more minutes, refilled our water bottles at a fountain, then got on our bikes and rode through the town.

After Órbigo, Marty got ahead of me. I rode by myself,

taking my time and enjoying the scenery. After a half-hour or so, I saw Marty waiting for me under a tree. We stopped, had some Peanut M&Ms, and then got back on the trail together.

"How ya feeling today, Jumbo?"

"Pretty good. No major back issues today, actually. You?"

"Feeling great," said Marty. "Nice to have some time to yourself out here, huh?"

"Yes it is," I said, breathing in the warm air.

"I ride by myself all the time back home." Of course, I knew this. Even before he retired, Marty had more free time than anyone else I have ever met.

Marty continued, "Lots of times I get into a conversation with myself while I'm riding. You ever do that?"

"You mean... out loud?"

"Yeah."

"Can't say I've ever done that."

"I do it all the time."

"How do those conversations go?"

"Usually really well. No arguments—it's a nice give-and-take. Just talking with myself about what's happening in my life. Getting to know myself better."

"How's it usually end?"

"After a while I realize that... well, you know... I'm a pretty good guy. And I look forward to our next conversation."

I shook my head, laughing, happy to know that Marty got along well with his most frequent riding companion.

28

THE DUET

HOSPITAL DE ÓRBIGO TO ASTORGA

"Jumbo!"

I hit the brakes and turned around.

"What?"

About 50 yards behind me, Marty had stopped his bike next to what looked like some sort of tent compound.

"Come back!" he called. "Check this out!"

All along the Camino, there are stands called *donativos* where locals leave out snacks or souvenirs, typically with a jar for donations. Marty had spotted a giant party-sized version—two big tents with chairs, sofas, a bed (yes, a bed), and several tables with fruit, nuts, olives, and crackers. Spanish guitar music was drifting from inside, and a dozen pilgrims were lounging about. It was right on the Camino—how did I miss it?

I rode back and joined Marty. We parked our bikes, entered one of the tents, got some fruit, and chatted with several of the pilgrims. Marty plopped into a cushy couch and put his feet up. Shade and chairs—*now* I understood why he wanted to stop.

We identified where the music was coming from. A man in his thirties, who looked to be in charge of the place, was fingerpicking an acoustic guitar. After he set down his instrument, I pointed at it. He held it up toward me.

"*Tú?*" he asked.

"Sí, gracias," I replied.

He handed me the guitar, and I began strumming a Crosby, Stills & Nash tune. He listened politely, but I could tell he didn't recognize it. Then again, it could have been my attempt at the song that made it unrecognizable.

"Do you know any American music?" I asked.

He didn't speak English, but he got the gist of what I was asking. Without saying anything, he went behind the tent and returned with a *second* guitar. He sat down next to me and started playing some chords. After a few bars, I recognized it—it was "The House of The Rising Sun" by the Animals! Not quite American, but close.

Guitar duet on the Camino

He motioned to me, and I began playing and singing along with him. Soon the other pilgrims gathered around, singing too. Afterwards, we celebrated with the universal language of a "high five." He told us his name was Kebben, or maybe it was Kevin? We took a picture, thanked him, and bid him farewell.

It was one of the most memorable moments of our entire Camino. And it wouldn't have happened had it not been for my artist brother-in-law, who never passes up a good couch.

WE RODE TOGETHER, enjoying the sunshine as the trail undulated through a vast, open area. We could see to the horizon in nearly every direction.

"How awesome is that, Jumbo? You got to play guitar on the Camino!"

"Never thought that would happen. Gotta be the highlight of the trip for me so far."

"Hey, when we get back, Belle and I want to finally throw a retirement party. Would you be willing to play and sing?"

"Sure, I'd love that."

"All our friends are retiring now," said Marty as we pedaled along. "Belle has so many colleagues from having taught at the same school for forty years. It seems like she's asking me to go to a retirement party with her just about every month."

I actually already knew this from having been in the room during a conversation at Belle and Marty's house a few months earlier. Here's how that went:

Belle: "Marty, we need to go to Elaine's retirement party this Saturday."

Marty: "Why, Belle? I was planning to go on a long ride that day."

Belle: "I worked with her for thirty years! It's a big deal, Marty. I need you to be willing go to these things with me."

Marty: "I do, Belle! Remember Charles' retirement party last February? I went to that one. Stayed the whole time."

Belle: "That was *in our house!*"

Marty: "So? I was there! It still counts, right?"

"Well, Marty, there are worse things than going to retirement parties. And I would be happy to play at yours."

Looking ahead, I spotted two cyclists stopped on the side of the Camino. "Hey, check out those guys."

One of the riders was working on his bike. He had the rear wheel off and was changing a flat tire. There was no tree cover —they were fully exposed to the sun. Marty and I pulled over.

"Can we help?" I asked. "Ayuda?"

"No. We're fine. Muchas gracias," he replied.

We waited another minute to make sure they were okay. Then we bid them a "Buen Camino" and continued riding.

"We're pretty lucky we haven't had any flat tires yet," Marty said as we rode along. I was pedaling just behind him.

"Yup, that was a rear flat—the worst kind."

A few hundred yards later, our luck ran out. I watched from behind as the rack above Marty's wheel suddenly disintegrated. The last remaining support bar cracked through, and the entire rack was dangling off to one side. His panniers were rubbing against his tire and were starting to catch in his spokes.

"Marty! Stop! Your rack!"

He stopped his bike and calmly inspected it. He then proceeded to use bungee cords, duct tape, and zip ties to bind what was left of the rack into place.

"Jumbo, remember when I rigged it on our first day? Well, you know what this is called? What I'm doing now?"

"What?"

"*Advanced* rigging."

"Looks more like life support."

Marty's "advanced" solution didn't last long, so he alternated between pushing his bike and taking short rides for the remaining five miles to Astorga. We would clearly need to figure out some other way to transport his bags the next day.

As Astorga came into view, we passed a hop growing farm. We picked a few of the buds and smelled them. From that point on, we had one-track minds... *necesito una cerveza!*

We made our way toward the city center, riding along the Roman stone walls that once surrounded the village. Rounding a corner, we found ourselves in front of the Astorga Cathedral, the centerpiece of the town. It's a spectacular building with flying buttresses connecting its central clock tower to towers on the right and left, each with a different design and made of different materials. Construction of the church spanned 300 years from the 15th to 18th centuries—the Spanish like their siestas, you know—so the structure combines Gothic, Renaissance, Baroque, and even Neoclassical architecture.

Just across from the cathedral, we located our Airbnb and met the owner, a woman in her eighties. She showed us a courtyard behind the building where we could store our bikes, then gave us the room key and pointed upward. Our room was four flights up, and there was no elevator. Clearly she had no intention of making the climb with us, nor did we expect it. We thanked her and slowly began the ascent, our thighs feeling each step after the day's strenuous ride.

Once we arrived at the top, we realized it was worth the effort. Our room and its balcony looked directly at the cathedral's façade, and we had a bird's-eye view of the rest of the town and the Galician mountains in the distance.

Marty and I showered, then immediately got to work figuring out what to do with his bags now that his rack was broken. In speaking with several pilgrims, we'd learned that many were shuttling their packs using baggage services. We walked to a nearby hotel and attempted to ask the owner how the shuttle works. He tried to explain, but it was no use.

View of Astorga Cathedral from our balcony

Seeing our frustration, he pulled out his phone, called someone, and spoke to them in Spanish. Once he was finished, he wrote "Jacotrans" and "Gaudi Hotel, 7:45 a.m." on a piece of paper. One more example of the helpful people in Spain.

We went to the Gaudi Hotel, directly across the street from Gaudi's Episcopal Palace, another building designed in the late 1800s by Antoni Gaudi. Inside the hotel, we confirmed that Jacotrans, the shuttle company, would pick up the bags the next morning and take them to our next destination, Villafranca del Bierzo, for twelve euros each. Even though my rack was still functioning, I decided it would be nice to have my bags shuttled as well.

With that problem solved, we had time to do a little sight-seeing. We noticed a smaller church near the cathedral—the

Iglesia de Santa Marta. In the third century, the local Roman proconsul persecuted Christians, forcing them to worship Roman gods. Marta, a fervent Christian virgin, repeatedly refused to comply. After being beaten and sent to prison, she was finally beheaded and is now honored as the patron saint of Astorga. We spent a few prayerful minutes inside the church.

Marty wanted to go back to the apartment to do some laundry, so I walked through the rest of the town on my own, looking for food for dinner. One store window stopped me in my tracks. A dozen different hams and sausages were hanging from the ceiling on strings. Looking up, the sign above the door read *"Charcuterie."* I stepped inside and was captivated by the array of meats and cheeses in the display cases. After some deliberation, I opted for Serrano ham, thinly sliced chorizo sausage, and Manchego cheese.

"Bread?" I asked the butcher as he rang up my total.

He shook his head. *"La panadería,"* he said, pointing down the street.

"Gracias." I paid for the food and headed out.

I walked a few blocks and found the bakery, which was just getting ready to close. Behind the counter were a few loaves baked that morning, along with a tray of flat bread cut into squares, with meat and cheese oozing from inside. I got the attention of the owner and pointed at them.

"Empanadas," she said.

"Dos," I said, holding up two fingers. "And one loaf of bread, por favor?"

As she was wrapping up my food, I realized I hadn't yet bought anything for dessert. Marty's blood sugar levels would be dangerously low tonight if I didn't come back with some kind of pastry. I looked around the bakery, but none were to be found.

"Pastry?" I asked.

"Pastelería," she said, motioning outside. I wasn't sure where

she was pointing, so she walked out the door with me. I followed her around a corner, down a block, and there it was—a pastry shop, also in the process of shutting down for the day.

"Muchas gracias!"

Nothing was left in the display cases, but sitting on the counter was a smaller version of the same pastry Marty had enthusiastically personified in León. This time the process was far easier—all I had to do was point. I bought two of them.

Back on the street, I passed a wine store, where I bought a bottle, and then a convenience store, where I found a couple of cans of cold beer and more Peanut M&Ms for tomorrow. Finally, after five stops, I had all I could carry. I slowly made my way toward our apartment.

At home in Pittsburgh, all of this would have been accomplished in a single trip to the Giant Eagle. At first, the American engineer in me was growing impatient with the inefficiency of the whole process. But as I walked along, I recalled that my Italian grandmother used to shop for dinner the very same way in her neighborhood in Bayonne, New Jersey. Each store had the best of what it specialized in, and she only wanted the best, even for an ordinary weeknight dinner. There was something perfectly satisfying about it.

As I got closer to our building, I saw two women walking toward me who looked familiar. I was sure I had met them before - but where?

"Hola! Good to see you, Jim!"

My brain finally kicked in. It was Shannon and Lorraine, whom we'd met at the tapas bar in Logroño.

"Wow, small world! Great to see you too!"

"How has your trip been? How's Marty?"

"He's good. Our trip has been... fantastic. Definitely some highs and some lows. Today was a high. But we've had a few tough days, too, and we had to get a lift a couple of times. I've been having some back problems."

"Oh, sorry to hear that."

"How about you? How did you manage to catch up with us? You must be speed walkers!"

"We took a bus across the whole meseta, from Burgos to León. Then we started walking again. We'll walk the rest of the way to Santiago."

Suddenly, I didn't feel so bad about having "cheated" and missed a few sections.

"Well, I gotta head back. Marty's waiting for dinner. Buen Camino!"

"Buen Camino!"

I carried the food to our apartment, ascended the stairs, and greeted Marty with the spoils of my shopping expedition.

Feast fit for a king on our balcony in Astorga

As I emptied the contents of each bag, Marty's eyes widened.

"Nice work, Jumbo!"

We set everything up on a table on our balcony, then proceeded to enjoy a sumptuous feast overlooking the cathedral.

While we were eating, at precisely 7:00 p.m., we were startled by seven deafening "GONGs" coming from the cathedral's bell tower in front of us. Another bell rang every fifteen minutes, followed by eight loud "GONGs" at 8:00, and again at 9:00 and 10:00. Would this continue all night?

Fortunately, 10:00 was the last one—the cathedral took a break until 8:00 the next morning. Marty and I slept well.

29

CRUZ DE FERRO
ASTORGA TO PONFERRADA

Picture this. A medieval village, surrounded by stone walls built over two millennia ago. Beyond the walls, green foothills. In the distance, layers of blue-gray mountain silhouettes. Above, a clear sky, with streaks of purple and orange as the sun starts its day over the horizon. In front, a 500-year-old cathedral. A top-floor balcony. A pastry. An espresso. And the only thing you have to do today is ride your bike.

Well, actually, one more thing. We had to pack up our bags and get them over to the Gaudi Hotel by 7:45 a.m.

We arrived a few minutes early. Dozens of other bags were already sitting in the lobby, each with an envelope attached labeled "Jacotrans." We grabbed two blank envelopes, wrote our names, phone numbers and destination on them, put the cash inside and attached them to our bags. I had an extra Apple AirTag, and at the last minute, I stuffed it in one of my panniers "just in case." Crossing our fingers, we left the bags there and walked back to our apartment.

I began making sandwiches from the previous evening's leftovers. As I was layering the meat and cheese on the bread,

Marty spotted a jar of mayonnaise in the refrigerator, likely left by a previous guest.

"Jumbo, could you put some of that mayo on mine?"

"I'm not sure that's a good idea. We'll be outside in the sun all day. This stuff could get warm."

"You know, everyone always says that about mayo. I don't get it. As soon as it goes in your body, it's immediately heated up to almost a hundred degrees. It's like your body *wants* it to be hot. I'll take my chances."

I shrugged and lathered Marty's sandwich with the mayonnaise.

"Do they have any other condiments here?" Marty asked.

I took another look in the refrigerator. "I don't see any."

"What about pickles?" Marty wasn't giving up.

"No pickles."

"Are pickles really a condiment, anyway?" Marty asked.

"I don't think so. I think a pickle is more of an *accoutrement*. It's on the side. Condiments are spreadable—like mayo, mustard, ketchup, hoagie spread..."

"What about thin-sliced pickle chips that go on a sandwich? Or lettuce and tomato? Onion?"

"I don't think those are condiments. They're all accoutrements," I said. "But *diced* onion—that would definitely be a condiment. So would relish."

"Who decides, anyway?" Marty asked.

"Well, I'll bet it's the big condiment companies—you know, Hellman's, Heinz, Hunt's," I said. "They probably all get together and have some sort of council. I'm sure Big Condiment wants to box out all the accoutrement companies to keep the industry from getting too competitive."

While others on the Camino were having deep conversations about the meaning of life, Marty and I were debating the nature of sandwich toppings.

Marty got our bikes set up, and when the cathedral bells

rang at 9:00 a.m., we were ready to go. Each of us had a light-weight bag containing a few things we might need during the day. I stuffed the sandwiches in my bag and strapped it to my rack.

The day's ride would be 50 miles with 3,150 feet of climbing. Around mid-day we would hit the highest elevation point of the entire Camino—about 5,000 feet—at the Cruz de Ferro (Iron Cross). We'd been anticipating it ever since watching "The Way." At the start of our day, we were about 160 miles from Santiago.

As we made our way uphill, now without our panniers, we immediately appreciated the reduced weight on our bikes. I was actually ahead of Marty during the entire ascent.

"Pinch yourself Jumbo!" Marty yelled.

"Riding our bikes—*in Spain!*" I responded.

As we headed west from Astorga, the landscape transitioned from the flat, rolling plains of the meseta to the lush, green mountains of Galicia (pronounced by the locals as "Galithia"). It looked like the Pacific Northwest, and a bit like Ireland, with cows grazing on the grassy hillsides.

We rode through several small medieval villages. The first was Rabanal del Camino, about twelve miles from Astorga, a typical stopping point for pilgrims on foot. With 1,200 feet of climbing behind us, we were still feeling pretty good. At Rabanal, we spotted a road adjacent to the Camino and decided to ride it for a stretch. It was steeper but far smoother, with spectacular views of the valley below.

Four miles later, we arrived at Foncebadón, just beneath the summit, and stopped for a break. This was a flourishing Camino village in the Middle Ages, supporting pilgrims with an albergue, a church, and even a hospital. When the Camino declined starting in the 16th century, the town was hit hard, and by 1990 it had only two inhabitants—a mother and son. In recent years, the influx of Camino pilgrims has led to a revitalization in Foncebadón, and many of its buildings have been renovated. It was a lively place on this beautiful morning.

At a café we met Laurie from Washington state, who had started walking the Camino with a friend in St. Jean Pied de Port. Unfortunately, she'd torn a tendon in her ankle just before Burgos, ending her "ambulatory" Camino. Her companion continued to walk the trail, while Laurie took a taxi to the stopping point each night. Of course, Laurie would arrive much earlier than her friend, giving her time to sit in cafés and meet other pilgrims. She said it wasn't the Camino experience she'd planned, but it had still been the trip of a lifetime and a very moving and spiritual journey for her.

Laurie was having an early lunch with Ronald from the Netherlands. The Dutch speak perfect English, and we had a nice conversation. Ronald said he'd met a man from Italy that morning who had walked the Camino *21 times*—twice each year. So far, we'd met a number of people who were "serial pilgrims," but this was in an entirely different league.

Marty and I had our passports stamped at the café, then mounted our bikes for the final ascent to the top.

Most walkers we'd seen on the Camino were carrying high-end backpacks, using trekking poles, and wearing moisture-wicking hiking clothes. But on our approach to the summit, we saw a lone man who looked to be in his seventies, dressed in a heavy brown long-sleeve shirt and gray pants. He was pulling a metal shopping cart full of clothes. Back in Pittsburgh, I might have taken him for a homeless person.

I was pedaling slowly behind him, watching him as he walked. He looked as if he were deep in thought.

That's gotta be brutal, pulling that cart over these rocks for 500 miles. His clothes must be soaked through with sweat. Why is he out here by himself? What compelled him to walk the Camino? What is going through his mind?

Man ascending from Foncebadón to the Cruz de Ferro

We passed the man and exchanged a "Buen Camino." As we ground our way uphill, I kept thinking about him. Knowing what was just ahead—the Iron Cross, where we would leave our stones as a symbol of releasing a burden—I began reflecting. *What burden would my stone represent?* The fact that I had to think hard about it was really telling.

I'd been blessed with a faith-filled, loving marriage to Katie for 35 years. We had three wonderful sons, an amazing daughter-in-law, and now a beautiful granddaughter. I had retired after a rewarding career and was now able to enjoy traveling, including this Camino trip. I still had my octogenarian mother —now a great-grandmother—along with my siblings and extended family as part of my life. And I had friends like Marty who would do anything for me. Yes, we had experienced loss over the past few years, with my dad and Katie's parents passing away. But we hadn't experienced a true tragedy—yet.

I continued to ponder this as we followed the ridge toward the summit and then rounded a bend.

We looked up—there it was.

Cruz de Ferro (Iron Cross)

In front of us, on top of a mound of rocks at least twenty feet high and 40 feet across, was the Iron Cross.

We parked our bikes and stepped slowly toward it. Two pilgrims were at the base of the cross, taking their time and placing their stones underneath. We waited for them to finish, then climbed up the rock pile ourselves.

Rising out of the mound was a sixteen-foot wooden pole topped with a five-foot metal cross. At its base were literally millions of stones, many with a word or two written on them—"cancer," "alcohol," "divorce," or the name of a lost loved one. Sometimes a longer message was written on a piece of paper attached to a stone. Around the bottom of the pole were pictures and mementos left as tributes to spouses, parents, children, and friends who had passed away. We saw all kinds of tokens—scarves, pins, toys, even a beer can.

There are several theories as to the origin of the cross. One is that it may have been erected to mark the Camino when it snows, as the path is frequently hidden in the winter at this elevation. Others believe the Celts originally marked this mountaintop with a stack of stones as a way of paying homage to their gods, and later the Christians replaced it with a cross. It's believed that the original cross was placed here in the early 11th century by the abbot of the lodgings at Foncebadón and Manjarín. That cross is now preserved in a museum in Astorga (the current cross is actually a replica).

We brought our stones out of the special bags which Belle had given to us and slowly placed them under the cross.

Marty and I each took some time to ourselves to reflect. While we were there, the man with the shopping cart completed his ascent, took a stone out of his pocket, placed it under the cross, and stood there for several minutes.

Being part of a centuries-old tradition, standing in the same spot as millions of other pilgrims over the past 1,000 years, overwhelmed us. It made me appreciate that everyone has something they're carrying with them—we just don't always see it.

. . .

AFTER A FEW MORE MINUTES, we got on our bikes. The road followed the Camino along a prominent ridge, with dramatic views of the Galician mountains in every direction. At this elevation, we were above the tree line, and the ground was covered with low-lying grass and scrub. The sky was blue, and the air was clean and crisp.

A few hundred yards later, we found a stunning overlook with some large boulders and decided it would be a good spot for lunch. We parked and sat down on the rocks. I brought out our sandwiches and handed the one with mayonnaise to Marty.

"Jumbo, thanks for making these."

"No prob—enjoy!" I bit into mine. The chorizo, ham and cheese were a perfect combination—and a nice break from Peanut M&Ms.

Marty looked at his sandwich before starting into it.

"Jumbo, I gotta tell you, nice work here with the diagonal cut." Marty pointed at how I had sliced his sandwich on an angle.

"Glad you like it," I said as I chewed.

"The diagonal cut is so much better than the vertical cut, isn't it? I really can't think of any situation where the vertical cut would be better."

"I didn't really think much about it, Marty. I just cut it."

"See, the thing about the vertical cut is... well... you know... you have this blunt edge coming right at you. And you end up getting stuff all over your face."

"I guess so..."

"But with the diagonal cut, see, it's clean. You have angles. You have options. Plus, it just looks so much classier, doesn't it? It's like... the Rolls Royce of sandwich cuts."

I laughed as Marty took his first bite.

"Wow, delicious, Jumbo. The Manchego cheese totally makes it," he said as he chewed.

I nodded.

"It's more exotic than, say, Swiss or provolone, isn't it?" Marty continued. "What's the deal with Swiss cheese, anyway? With all those holes? You need to use twice as many slices to get the same coverage. Or you end up with a bite with no cheese."

"True."

"The Swiss... they do a lot of things right. You know... watches, army knives, chocolate..."

"Bank accounts..."

"Yeah, and those Little Debbie cake rolls too. But they just can't seem to get cheese right. It doesn't make sense. They're known for such precision in everything else, but their cheese is full of holes. I don't think it's an oversight. It's like they're intentionally trying to get away with something."

"That's gotta be it. By the way, how's that mayo tasting?"

"Great, Jumbo. You don't know what you're missing."

We munched on our sandwiches, enjoying the view.

"Awesome experience—that cross—huh, Marty?"

"Sure was."

"So, I know it's personal, but I suppose I can guess the burden you tried to let go of up there. It's been... how many days now?" I grinned and looked at Marty.

Marty chuckled. "I wish it was as easy as tossing a rock, Jumbo. Doesn't work that way for me, unfortunately."

Marty paused, then asked, "How about you, Jumbo?"

"Seeing all those names and pictures made me realize how lucky we are."

"I know," said Marty. "Seems like a lot of people we've met on the trail have something big they're going through."

"Yeah. So as I laid down my stone, I decided to do it for all of those people. And for whatever burdens may happen in the future for us. I know they'll come."

Marty and I sat there in silence, continuing to take in the view. As we were finishing our lunch, a giant tour bus pulled in to the area where we'd left our bikes, and two dozen German tourists poured out, pointing at the view. I guess we'd picked a popular spot. We took that as our signal to head out.

Just before we left, I remembered our bags. We had felt a little uncomfortable just leaving them in the Gaudi Hotel lobby, never having used a shuttle service before. I opened up the "Find My" app on my phone and was relieved to see that the bags had already reached our next destination, Villafranca del Bierzo!

Our minds at rest and our stomachs full, we got back on the road, pedaling easily for another few hundred yards along on the ridge. At that point, the incline changed.

Gravity. It's a funny thing. You don't really think about it, but it's always there. Rollercoasters are designed to take advantage of it. The large 'coasters all start out the same. A chain pulls you up a big hill. Then, as you crest the top, the chain lets go. There's that brief moment when you're barely moving, and you take in the view of the whole amusement park. Then, your car points downward, and gravity takes over. You don't really notice the view after that. It's an indescribable adrenaline rush, and afterwards, you want to do it again.

After slowly climbing nearly 3,000 feet over twenty miles in the morning, then gliding along the ridge top and enjoying the view for a mile or so, Marty and I bombed down 3,000 feet over only ten miles. The road made a winding descent into the valley, leading us through one hairpin bend after another. As our speed approached 40 mph, I lowered my seat using my dropper post* and rode the brakes, the wind buffeting my face and whipping past my ears. I felt like a downhill slalom skier, shifting my weight and leaning into each turn. Calling on all

---

* A dropper post allows you to adjust the height of your seat while riding. It's activated using a lever on the handlebars. Lowering the seat on descents allows for better control and increased safety. I had no idea my bike had this feature until Marty showed me.

my senses, I focused every ounce of mental and physical energy on trying not to crash.

It was the longest, fastest, scariest, and most exhilarating descent either of us had ever experienced. The whole trip down took only 30 minutes. It would take those on foot an entire day. I'm sure there was magnificent scenery all around us, but I didn't see any of it.

The road led us through the small mountain village of El Acebo and then crossed the Meruelo River into Molinaseca. The town was silent, except for the sound of birds singing. We stopped for a minute to catch our breath and listen.

"Jumbo! That was awesome!"

"Incredible! I have never gone that fast. No cars even passed us!"

"Check this out." Marty reached down and touched his brake rotor. "This thing is white hot. If there was any clay left in our brakes, I think we melted it away."

The descent finally ended once we reached Ponferrada, a mid-sized town of about 60,000 people. We followed the Camino through the city, then rounded a corner and were stunned by what we saw. It was a massive medieval castle, complete with a moat, drawbridge, turrets, and flags flying at the top. It looked like something out of "Shrek" or "The Princess Bride," and we fully expected to see a damsel in distress leaning out the top window with her braided hair dangling down the side.

This was the Castle of the Knights Templar, a military order founded by the French in 1119. The Knights' original charter was to defend pilgrims on their way to Jerusalem, and they were endorsed by the Catholic Church in 1129. This endorsement enabled them to seek donations and gifts, leading to the development of their own banking system and extensive land holdings. They were skilled fighters and warriors, protecting the Church as well as European kings and queens, and figuring prominently in the Crusades.

When the Camino grew in popularity as a Christian pilgrimage route during the Middle Ages, the Knights Templar protected pilgrims on the Way, and this castle was built in 1178 as their regional headquarters. It's an impressive and imposing fortress which now houses the 1400-volume Templar library.

Marty and I toured the outside of the castle, had our passports stamped, and got back on our bikes to complete our final fifteen-mile leg of the day to Villafranca del Bierzo. The weather was perfect—we would be there in time for a relaxing dinner.

Knights Templar Castle in Ponferrada

30

THE SUB-PAR SOFT SERVE
PONFERRADA TO VILLAFRANCA DEL BIERZO

A fter Ponferrada, the terrain leveled out. We rode through an area of vineyards, apple groves, and hop farms toward Villafranca del Bierzo. The waning late afternoon sun was making its way over the mountains to the west. Marty was just behind me, and as we rode through the countryside, I began to daydream and think about all we had done and seen that day.

This had been a very challenging day, but I was surprised and pleased that the 3,000 feet of climbing had not wiped me out. I reflected on our training over the last few months and was glad we had ridden a lot of hills to prepare for the trip. I was also glad I'd done some mountain biking, as it is quite different from rail-trail riding.

∽

SOME OF OUR training had occurred in the Bavington State Gamelands, Marty's favorite mountain biking spot near Pittsburgh. One Sunday in May, Marty and I went there with his friend, Jack. We got a workout in the woods, riding twenty miles with over 3,000 feet of climbing.

After the ride, in the parking lot, Marty pulled three folding chairs out of his car. Jack and I sat down as Marty continued rummaging through his trunk.

"Hey, Jim," said Jack. "Marty and I are thinking of riding at Raystown Lake next weekend. Wanna come?"

"Marty was telling me about that place—we were talking about going at some point this summer. But I can't make it next weekend. Katie and I have plans."

"Do you mind if we go ahead without you?" asked Jack. "It's the only free weekend I have for the next month."

"It's cool. You and Marty go ahead." I said. "He and I have agreed it's good for us to bike with other people. We have an open biking relationship." We both laughed.

Marty was still rifling through the back of his car. "Hey, guys, I have some bad news."

"What?" I asked.

"I forgot to bring beer."

I was shocked. Marty may not remember to buy gifts for his family at Christmas or bring pants to a graduation*, but he always remembered to bring beer to a bike ride.

"How about ice cream instead? Jumbo, did we ever take you to the Robinwood Diner?"

"No, where is it?" I asked.

"It's right on the way back. We stop there a lot—we can get a soft serve."

Jack and I nodded in agreement. "Let's do it."

---

* In the original "Get Up and Ride" book, the chapter entitled "No User Fee" explains how Marty bought a pair of pants to wear to a graduation—and then returned them the next day. When asked by the clerk whether there was anything wrong with them, his reply was: "No, I just don't need them anymore."

Also, as mentioned in Chapter 20, Marty gives his children paper IOU's as Christmas presents.

We quickly packed up our things and drove to the Robin-wood. It was a classic old-time diner with padded stools lining the counter. The cook was in the back huddled over the grill. I spotted the soft serve machine and the milkshake spinner beside it. All good signs.

It was crowded, and a line had formed in front of each of the two cash registers. The first line was being served by a heavyset woman—it was a bit longer and seemed to be moving slowly. The second line was tended by a slender teenage girl—it was moving faster. I was hot, thirsty, and hungry, so I immediately took my place at the end of the shorter line. Marty chose the other line, and Jack joined him. I wondered what they were up to.

Marty cupped his hand to his mouth. "Hey Jumbo, come over here," he said in a loud whisper as he motioned to me.

"Why?" I asked. "This line is moving faster."

"Just come over here and I'll tell you."

I reluctantly joined them. "What's up, Marty?"

Marty leaned toward me and spoke in a low voice. "Jumbo, look at who's working these two lines. That skinny girl over there, and this, well, kinda big lady over here. Think about it. Who's gonna make you the larger cone?"

"Don't they have set portions?"

"Well *theoretically*, yeah, but there's a lot of leeway, right?"

"Okay..." I stammered. The line was inching very slowly towards the counter. The other line continued to outpace ours. We finally reached the front.

"Three large vanilla cones," said Marty.

The woman slowly made her way to the soft serve machine. She picked up a cone and placed it under the dispenser. After filling the cone's base, she made one circular motion after another, adding layer upon layer as she built a massive, creamy, white tower. She added the finishing touch—a swirl on the top —then swung the handle closed, turned around, and handed the enormous cone to Marty. We all nodded at each other in approval.

She proceeded to make two more cones exactly the same way. We paid for them, took them outside, and sat down at a picnic table.

Knowing we would need to consume them quickly before they melted, we dove into our cones immediately.

"Uh, huh!! How 'bout this?!" exclaimed Marty. "Ever see a cone that big, Jumbo?"

"Yeah baby!" said Jack, licking his ice cream.

The chill of the frozen confection in my mouth provided immediate relief after sweating for two hours on the trails. Then, after the first few licks, my taste buds kicked in. I stopped eating and looked at my cone. There was something missing.

"Do you guys *like* this soft serve?" I asked.

"Do we *like* this soft serve?" Marty said mockingly, looking at Jack. "What kind of question is that?"

"I mean, do you guys really like this?"

Marty realized I was being serious. "Jack and I have stopped here dozens of times over the years. Always get the soft serve. What's wrong?"

My ice cream was melting as I held it out toward them.

"This is not good soft serve," I declared.

"What??" said Marty in shock. They continued devouring their cones.

"I mean, guys, it's just not good." I reiterated.

"Isn't all soft serve basically the same stuff?" asked Jack. "Don't they all use the same bag of powder and pour it in the machine the same way?"

"Well, I don't know how it's made, but I do know soft serve, and I know what I like. And this is inedible."

I stood up and walked over to the garbage can. A swarm of bees was circling around the top. I quickly opened the hinged door and tossed in my cone. I returned to Marty and

Jack at the picnic table. Both of them looked at me in disbelief.

"Jumbo, you just threw out a perfectly good cone. Oversized, too. Who *does* that?"

"If it was perfectly good, I wouldn't have thrown it out."

Marty and Jack stopped eating and stared at their cones. Jack slowly got up from the table, stepped over to the garbage can, and tossed in his cone.

Marty took one more lick, then looked up at us. He shook his head, slapped his hand on the table, and got up in a huff. He walked over to the trash can and threw in his cone.

"You happy, Jumbo?" Marty said, clearly upset.

"What?" I pleaded.

"We've been coming here for years, and all this time I thought I was eating good soft serve. You've now ruined this place for us."

"Sorry, Marty, I gotta call it like I see it. Life's too short to eat bad soft serve."

We said our goodbyes and headed home.

Marty and his friends kept biking at Bavington nearly every Sunday. But they never went back to the Robinwood. Before long, the diner closed down, which didn't surprise me in the least.

A FEW WEEKS LATER, Marty and I did a training ride on the Great Allegheny Passage rail-trail. Midway through our ride, we stopped at the Outflow Soft Freeze in Confluence, PA. We each ordered a large vanilla cone and sat down at a table outside. Marty watched me carefully as I took my first lick, and then a second.

"You're not eating?" I asked.

"Not yet," said Marty, continuing to watch me as I ate.

"Well, Jumbo?" Marty asked.

"What?"

"How is it?"

"Whaddya mean?"

"Is it good soft serve?" asked Marty.

"Try it for yourself," I said, motioning to his cone.

Marty took a lick. "Well, before that day at the Robinwood, I would have said it was good. But... I really don't know anymore. Now I'm always questioning my own judgement. You've tainted the entire soft serve experience for me."

"Marty, let me assure you... *this* is good soft serve."

"Whew!" Marty was relieved.

MARTY CONTINUES TO TRY TO "CURE" himself of his constant questioning of soft serve. As for me, since that day, I've had plenty of sub-par burgers, pizza, wings, and even beer when I'm with Marty, but I've learned to keep quiet and let him think he's enjoying it.

31

SOLITUDE
VILLAFRANCA DEL BIERZO

"**S**olitary confinement," said Evan.

"How long?" I asked.

"Sixteen years."

"Are you serious?!"

"Yup. No contact with the other inmates. No letters to or from my family or friends. No phone calls."

"Is that typical?"

"Not at all. Look, I made a big mistake when I was eighteen. They gave me a life sentence. Three years in, I tried to escape. I figured I'd either get away or get killed. I was good with it either way. I didn't think about the third option. They caught me and put me in the hold."

"You're out of there now? In a regular cell?"

"Yeah, been in a regular cell for ten years. I've been down twenty-nine years now."

Evan was an inmate in a maximum security state correctional institution in Pennsylvania, home to 1,500 men, 140 of whom were on death row. It was June 2023, three months before our Camino trip. I was part of a team leading a four-day Christian retreat program inside the prison, and Evan and I were seated at a table eating lunch.

"How were you able to survive sixteen years in there? I would have gone insane."

"One thing they did let me have was a Bible. I read it cover to cover—ten times. I found God in that cell. And I eventually found forgiveness."

WE'D STARTED the day in Astorga, at the edge of the meseta, and were ending in the region of El Bierzo, in the Galician mountains. Over the course of eight hours and 50 miles, the terrain and climate had completely changed—from flat, brown, and arid to hilly, green, and moist. We had 115 miles to go to Santiago.

The Romans first discovered gold in these hills over 2,000 years ago. They proceeded to dig the largest open-pit gold mine in the entire Roman Empire in nearby Las Médulas, now a UNESCO World Heritage site.

This was an astonishing feat of engineering. The Romans used aqueducts to redirect stream water into a reservoir, then built channels to blast the water at the mountains, removing the soil and exposing the gold.

Naturally, at the end of a long day of blasting and mining, the Romans liked to relax with a little vino. So they started cultivating grapes here, too.

Later, in the ninth century, the Cistercian monks settled in El Bierzo, built a monastery (which still stands), and expanded the winemaking operation. Apparently, monks liked to drink wine, too, but they also sold it to support themselves. Over the years, winemaking grew into a large enterprise in the area. As with all profitable businesses, the wineries paid taxes.

The Moors arrived here about the same time the Camino

was getting started. The king at the time recognized that the Way of St. James was bringing in Christians from all over Europe. Wanting to build up the local population to keep the Moors away, he made it attractive for people to settle in the village. *Villafranca del Bierzo* means "Free Village of El Bierzo"—people could stay and live here tax-free.

Marty and I pedaled into Villafranca, our stop for the night. We picked up our bags at the hotel where Jacotrans had left them, then rode to our hotel, passing medieval churches and historic buildings along the cobbled streets. The rough road jostled our bodies and bikes, each bump reminding my lower back that it was time for some Advil. We checked in and got cleaned up. I popped two tablets and we headed outside.

Villafranca del Bierzo was called "Little Compostela" in the Middle Ages. Pilgrims who were sick or in pain and unable to make the rest of the trip to Santiago de Compostela could (and still can) walk through the *Puerta del Perdón* ("Door of Forgiveness") into the Iglesia de Santiago to receive their indulgence. This was the only place on the Camino—other than the Santiago de Compostela Cathedral—where the indulgence could be given, and pilgrims still had to produce evidence of having walked at least 100 km (62 miles) via their passports.

Marty and I walked up to the Puerta del Perdón. It was a large, wooden, arched entryway on the side of the church which is now open only during Holy Years*. Given the shape my body was in, if the door had been opened that day, I may have called it quits and stepped through it myself.

---

* A "Holy Year" or "Jubilee Year" is a special year in Roman Catholic tradition in which followers are called to deepen their faith and perform works of charity. They can also receive special indulgences for their sins. "Ordinary" Holy Years have occurred every 25 years since the year 1300. The Pope can also proclaim an "extraordinary" Jubilee Year outside of the regular cycle to celebrate a major event or address a specific issue.

The year 2025 is an ordinary Jubilee Year with the theme "Pilgrims of Hope," encouraging pilgrimages to holy sites.

Puerta del Perdón (Door of Forgiveness)

As I looked at the Door of Forgiveness, I reflected back to the Hill of Forgiveness. The stones lying at the Iron Cross. The prisoners in the Middle Ages, working off their sentences on the Camino. And Craig in solitary confinement in Pennsylvania.

Marty and I were on a fun adventure. But in medieval times, this trip was not about fun—it was about suffering in search of forgiveness and healing. Craig found it by spending sixteen years in solitude. Over the centuries, many have also found it by spending a month or two on the Camino, with hours of solitude each day. With the constant barrage of TV, cell phone notifications, Zoom calls, and texts in today's world, silence is so elusive. And while the camaraderie with other pilgrims is certainly a big part of the Camino, it's in the solitude and silence that the magic happens. I was starting to understand why Marty likes to ride with himself so much.

Just across the street from the church was the Castillo Palacio de los Marqueses de Villafranca, a massive fortified palace built in 1515. It's still inhabited by the descendants of the Marqueses of Villafranca, a Spanish noble family whose roots trace to the 1400s.

Next to the castle was a restaurant—Café Bar el Castillo. It was a lively, casual place with a number of pilgrims having dinner outside at picnic tables. We found an open spot and began chatting with some of them.

Café Bar el Castillo, overlooking the Marqueses de Villafranca Castle

Throughout our entire trip, we'd been meeting pilgrims

who had experienced a brutal rain storm in the first week of September. It had occurred just before we started our trip and resulted from a hurricane which affected a wide swath of Spain. The section of the Camino between Pamplona and the Hill of Forgiveness had been flooded, and the small stream we'd seen running across the path had turned into a deep, fast-moving river during that time.

Authorities closed down that part of the Camino until it subsided; however, because many pilgrims were already on it, rescue teams were dispatched. We had spoken with two pilgrims in Astorga who said they'd walked from Pamplona to the Hill of Forgiveness, but due to the deluge and high water, they turned around and walked all the way back to Pamplona.

At the café in Villafranca, we chatted with Sophia, Ellen, and Richard, from the U.K., who were in that flood. Sophia was a marketer in the film industry in London, which she said is a nonstop, hectic, and stressful job (i.e. the "old me"). She told them she wanted to quit to walk the Camino, and they offered her a leave of absence instead. So she was off work until November, clearing her head and figuring things out.

"What's been the most memorable experience you've had on the Camino so far?" I asked the group.

"Saving someone's life," answered Sophia.

Marty and I leaned in.

"We were hiking up the Hill of Forgiveness and saw a woman with a backpack who was in chest-deep water and was being pulled under. The three of us ran down the bank, then made a human chain with Richard wading into the water and the two of us holding onto him. He grabbed her as she floated by and pulled her out."

"Jeez! Was she okay?"

"She was soaked, of course, but we were all soaked from the rain, anyway. We sat down with her for a while to make sure she was alright."

"Did that end her trip?"

"For that day, yes. She walked back to Pamplona, dried out, and got back on the trail after the rains ended. We pressed on. She's a few days behind us, but we keep in touch on our cell phones."

"Wow."

After dinner and a quick passport stamp, Marty and I took a stroll around town as dusk gave way to night. Rounding a corner, we discovered the Plaza Mayor, the main plaza in the center of town with a large outdoor bar. The place was buzzing with dozens of pilgrims. We got a couple of beers and walked past several tables, hoping to hear a conversation in English we might be able to join. *Bingo*—we found a table of four English speakers with two open seats and joined them.

We introduced ourselves. Tom and Allison were from Ireland, although they didn't know each other before the trip. Anna was from Israel, and Matthew was from Austria. They had all become friends on the Camino. Tom was the youngest of the group and looked to be in his early twenties. He had a notebook on the table in front of him—he said he was keeping a journal of his trip. Each evening he would write some of the noteworthy things that happened that day.

As we chatted, the conversation led to a discussion about music. I mentioned that I occasionally play acoustic Irish music, and before long, Allison, Tom, and I were singing together. We belted out "Fields of Athenry" in three-part harmony, followed by the classic "Danny Boy." After the final verse, we toasted our glasses as others around us clapped and cheered.

"That was fun!" I exclaimed.

"Would have been even better with Guinness in these glasses!" said Allison with a wink.

"So, Tom, will our singing make your journal today?" I beamed, pointing at his book.

"I'm not sure," he replied.

"Really?" I was surprised, and a little disappointed.

"Well, that *was* pretty good," admitted Tom. "But a lot of other good things happened today. And the night's not over. We'll see."

At least he was honest.

32

TORTILLAS
VILLAFRANCA DEL BIERZO

I opened my eyes after a good night's sleep. On most days, I had awakened first, and I assumed Marty was still in bed. I headed for the bathroom—the door was locked.

After another minute, Marty emerged with a smile on his face. "The eagle has landed!" he exclaimed, pumping his fist. "That one counted. Sorry you had to wait this morning, Jumbo."

"Maybe leaving that rock at the cross worked, huh?"

"Maybe. Or maybe my body just finally relented."

With rain in the forecast, my back aching, and my legs sore from the strenuous ride the previous day, I suggested to Marty that we hang out in Villafranca del Bierzo for the morning and get a ride in the afternoon to Sarria, our next destination. Marty said he felt good, having lightened his load a bit, but he knew I was hurting and agreed.

We walked back to the Café Bar el Castillo and sat at a table outside, with a stunning view of the castle. Looking over the breakfast menu, a picture of an omelet caught our eye. Marty was squinting, trying to read the words above the picture.

"What's this say, Jumbo?"

"*Tortilla.*"

"It looks like an omelet. Why are they calling it a tortilla?"

I Googled it on my phone.

"It says here that in Spain, a *tortilla* is an omelet filled with potatoes. In Mexico, it's a round, flat bread—the kind we're used to."

"Why is it different? Wasn't Mexico settled by Spain?"

"Yeah, it was. I don't know why."

"Well, here's what I think," said Marty, clearly about to answer to his own question. "I think *tortilla* started out in Spain meaning flat bread, too."

"Okay..."

"Yeah, the Spanish were all happy over here, rolling their burritos, enjoying their wraps. Then they took the tortilla to Mexico, and everyone loved it there, too. But then, I think Spain got jealous. Mexico had it a little too good, you know, with their gold and their silver, their beaches in Cancún, and what not. So the Spanish came up with something better—this omelet here. And they gave it the same name just to mess with the Mexicans."

"That is absolutely what happened," I said. "You need to take this to the international linguistics or anthropology experts. This is Nobel Prize stuff."

We were still laughing as our waitress approached our table. We ordered tortillas and espressos. Minutes later, she brought out our omelets—they were delicious. The Spanish were on to something here.

While we ate, I looked up a taxi service and called to make a reservation.

"Hola," said a man's voice on the other end.

"Hola. Habla Inglés?" I asked, hopefully.

"No."

"Taxi?"

"*Sí. Donde?*"

"Uhhh... one o'clock." I thought he was asking what time we wanted to be picked up.

"*Donde?*" he repeated.

I pulled the phone away from my ear. "*Donde?*" I asked Marty.

Our waitress saw me struggling and immediately offered to help, reaching for my phone. I handed it to her.

"Where do you want to be picked up?" she asked.

"How about right here? Around one o'clock," I said.

She engaged in a rapid-fire explosion of Spanish, cramming in more syllables per second than I have ever heard in any language. She returned my phone and declared, "It's booked! He'll be here at one."

Yet another Camino Angel.

While the omelets were delicious and filling, Marty still needed something else—a pastry. We paid our bill, then began walking around the town in the morning mist. We passed two impressive churches—the Iglesia de San Nicolas El Real and the Iglesia de San Francisco (St. Francis)—as well as the enormous Convent de Anunciada, also attributed to the Order of St. Francis. The streets were oddly deserted. Where was everyone?

Just then, we heard a voice from behind us. "Hola! Buenos dias!"

We turned around to see a man in a rain jacket, holding a pair of tongs and a garbage bag. On his backpack was a hand-made sign that read "Xcompasion."

"Hola," said Marty. "Walking the Camino today?"

"Yes! I'm José." He extended his hand with a big smile.

We shook hands and introduced ourselves. "What is Xcompasion?" I asked.

"I walk the Camino every year. My mission is keeping it

clean and showing others how to help the earth by reducing pollution. I pick up trash along the way and carry it to the next town. I have a YouTube channel where I promote it, too."

"Wow, all by yourself?" said Marty.

"It's my passion. How about you two?"

"We're biking the Camino. But taking a break today," I said.

"Ahh. Enjoy your day off. This is a nice town."

Marty chimed in, "Now that I think about it, José, we really haven't seen any garbage on the Camino since we started in Pamplona. It's so clean we could almost eat off it." Marty looked at me and smirked. "Is there really much litter out there? Or is a lot of it just debris?" Another smirk.

"Well, you guys must have come through after I'd already cleaned it up!" said José with a wink. "But seriously, half a million people are on the Camino this year. There's definitely a lot of garbage."

"There aren't any groups or local governments that do this?" I asked.

"Nope. Just me and a few others like me. One couple did the same thing on the Camino Portuguese a few years ago—they picked up 6,000 pieces of garbage."

"Hard to believe people would just throw trash on the trail," said Marty. "But thanks for what you're doing, José. The Camino is pristine!"

"Okay, amigos, I'm on my way to O Cebreiro. Adios! Buen Camino!"

We said goodbye and watched him head toward the Camino in the drizzle.

The brief conversation with José hadn't distracted Marty from his pastry quest. After walking a few more blocks, we found a café that didn't have pastries, but instead served the local confection—churros and chocolate. The "chocolate" is actually a cup of hot chocolate with the consistency of pudding and is heavenly. We dipped our churros and watched as the staff worked furiously behind the bar, making churros, brewing coffee, washing dishes, and serving food.

Churros and chocolate in Villafranca del Bierzo

"Look at how busy everyone is here, Jumbo. It's a nonstop flurry of activity... and it's making me dizzy."

"Marty, I think compared to you, everyone looks busy. Even a snail would look busy."

Marty smiled. "Maybe so, but I wish they would slow down. I'm getting tired just watching them."

We made our way back to our Airbnb, where we retrieved our bikes and bags and took them over to the Café Bar el Castillo to wait for our taxi. We chatted with a few pilgrims who were having lunch.

Naturally, the conversation was about blisters. One woman at the café said she'd gotten one on her first day in the Pyrenees. She said she popped it and then put plaster on it. She hadn't had any issues since then.

One guy showed us his foot—he was wearing a type of cotton "glove" that goes over each toe and up to his calves. This was the first we'd seen of such a creative and aggressive approach. I suppose the next step would be amputation.

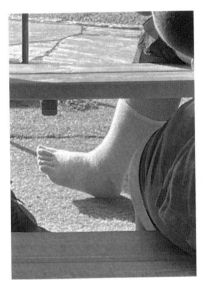

Creative blister-avoidance strategy in Villafranca del Bierzo

It would have felt like gloating to tell them we don't get blisters while riding on bikes—or in a taxi, for that matter—so we didn't say anything.

33

MARTY'S MEMORY
VILLAFRANCA DEL BIERZO TO SARRIA

W hen our taxi arrived, we said goodbye to the pilgrims at the café. We loaded our bikes in the back and began the ride to Sarria.

Leaving Villafranca, the road became very steep, and the driver turned on his windshield wipers to clear the mist and drizzle. As we approached O Cebreiro at the summit, we asked him if he could stop and let us check out the village.

We got out of the taxi and walked around. You may recall from Chapter 2 that O Cebreiro was the home of Father Elias Valiña Sampedro, the modern-day founder of the Camino who passed away in 1989. It's a tiny mountaintop settlement with fewer than 100 residents, but many pilgrims were out in the streets, sitting in the cafés, and browsing the souvenir shops.

It was much wetter and cooler at this elevation than in Villafranca, and the air was heavy with the smell of wood smoke. It had the feel of Ireland and looked like a scene from "The Hobbit," with round, stone houses topped with thatched roofs. We stepped into one of them and found the source of the smoke—a warm fire crackling on the floor. In the Middle Ages, these two-room huts would typically house about a dozen people and their animals. We were standing in the living area, where cooking was done over the fire and chorizo was smoked by hanging it from the ceiling above.

O Cebreiro

Just down the street we found the village church, Santa Maria Real, built into the ground to protect it from the notoriously harsh weather on this mountain. Founded in 836, it's the oldest church on the entire French Way.

It is said that on a snowy, windy winter night in the 14th century, a priest was celebrating Mass here alone. To his surprise, a peasant from a nearby village came in, wanting to receive Holy Communion. The priest was not a strong believer in the real presence of Christ in the Eucharist, and he scolded the man for walking through the blizzard just for "a piece of bread and some wine." However, during the consecration, the priest was stunned to see that the bread and wine had physically turned into flesh and blood, staining the linens on the altar red. News of the miracle spread quickly and even attracted the attention of King Ferdinand and Queen Isabella. The royal couple traveled to the site and donated a silver reliquary, which still holds the stained linens in a special shrine near the church.

Marty and I got back into the taxi and continued to head west. At the top of the next mountain (Alto de San Roque), our driver stopped to let us see the Pilgrim Monument, a colossal bronze statue of a pilgrim braving the wind on the summit. Some pranksters with a sense of humor had put Band Aids on the statue's heels to make it look authentic.

Pilgrim Monument, Alto de San Roque

Our taxi then headed down the other side of the mountain. As we drove along, I lamented that we'd skipped yet another section of the Camino due to my body not cooperating. And I marveled at how Marty, five years older and 60 pounds heavier than me, was still feeling no ill effects from the challenging ride. In fact, for decades, Marty's only known physical frailties were the two issues mentioned earlier. Recently, however, he's admitted to a third challenge that's becoming increasingly apparent with age—his memory.

∾

MARTY IS VERY self-aware and has created compensating mechanisms which enable him to survive (and even thrive) in today's modern world. For example, since he doesn't have a calendar or a watch, he surrounds himself with people who have these devices—Belle, for one, and me, for another.

When I need to know if Marty is available on a certain date, I call Belle. If I were to call Marty, he would always say "yes," and when the date would arrive, he'd call and tell me about the conflict, and I would become frustrated. I have found that working directly with Belle is a far better approach.

When I once asked Marty how he keeps track of doctor appointments without a calendar, he simply said:

"They always call you the day before to remind you, don't they? I've never missed one."

In early June, as we were ramping up our training for the Camino journey, Marty began having chronic pain in his mouth. His long-time dentist wasn't able to fully address the issue, so he found a different dentist.

"How'd you decide on the new dentist?" I asked.

"A friend initially recommended him. On my first appointment, I sat down in the chair, and while he was putting on his gloves, I said, 'Doctor, before you start, I need to ask you something.'

'Yes?' he said.

'Does your office call patients the day before to remind them of their appointments?'

'Yes, we do.'

'Okay, let's do this!' I said."

Having carefully vetted his new dentist, Marty began a series of appointments, which ultimately led to extensive oral surgery in July. This sidelined him for a little while. During his recovery, I paid him a visit and brought him a milkshake. He was clearly uncomfortable and told me about the three different medications he needed to take over a ten-day period.

While we were sitting in his family room, the alarm on his phone went off. I was surprised, as I didn't think Marty knew the phone had an alarm, much less how to use it. Marty silenced it, grabbed a bottle of pills, tossed one in his mouth, and washed it down with the milkshake.

"Marty, you have the timing for all three medications programmed into your phone? I'm impressed."

"Well," said Marty sheepishly. "Belle did it."

We all know that Marty plans to go first. But if Belle happens to go first, God help us.

When I retired, I suggested to Marty that perhaps a good way for me to learn to really relax would be to ditch my calendar. That way I would be able to live more in the moment and potentially approach the level of "chill" which Marty seems to achieve so effortlessly. Marty thought for minute.

"Actually, Jumbo, I *don't* think that's a good idea. Keep the calendar."

"Why?"

"Well, you know how I sometimes lose track of days?"

"Marty, losing track days would imply that at one point you actually *had* track of days."

Marty laughed. "That's true. But if *you* don't have a calendar, when we have something planned, how will I know what day it is? Like... how will I know when we're supposed to go to Spain if it's not on your calendar?"

"Good point." I kept the calendar.

Three weeks later, Marty and Belle were over for dinner. Marty told me about a new compensating tool he was using to help him deal with his memory loss. On his rides, he began bringing a pad and pen to write down observations, conversations, or thoughts that he might want to remember.

He told me about his first ride with the pad and pen, which had occurred a few days before. Toward the end of his ride, he stopped at a traffic light. While he was waiting, another biker pulled up next to him. They struck up a conversation, and he started telling Marty about some great bike trips he'd taken around the country.

"There's one in particular you should check out. It's in Ohio. I'll tell you the website," said the cyclist.

"Hey, I appreciate it... but I gotta tell you, I have a really bad memory, and I won't remember it," admitted Marty.

"You know, I have the same problem. But I recently read an article about some tricks you can do to help remember things, and even improve your memory. They really work."

The man began rattling off these techniques, some of which sounded excellent to Marty. Just then, he remembered his pad and pen. He reached around to his shirt-back pocket to grab them.

I asked Marty, "So, you wrote some of these tricks down?"

"Well, I tried to, but by the time I got my pad out, he'd finished talking."

"But do you think some of them could be helpful for you?"

"Oh, for sure."

"Okay, so what was just one of them? Like... the best one?"

"I don't remember."

34

THE CAMINO GALS
SARRIA

O ur taxi wound its way down the mountain toward Sarria. As we passed through the village of Samos, we saw a bridal party standing outside near the sixth-century Monastery of San Xulián. I broke the silence.

"Marty, I remember you telling me about a wedding in Wisconsin you and Belle are going to this fall. A friend of Belle's from college, I think? I want to make sure it doesn't conflict with a GAP Trail event we've been invited to. That wedding is coming up pretty soon, right? "

"Yeah, I think so."

"When?"

"I don't know, Jumbo."

"Is it soon after we get back? Like October?"

"You'd have to ask Belle. I really have no idea."

"It *is* this fall, right? Not next spring?"

Marty thought for a few moments. "I do know this, Jumbo. It's in the future. It's not in the past. It hasn't happened yet."

I shook my head. Believe it or not, this was progress.

Ten minutes later, we arrived in Sarria. The driver dropped us off at our Airbnb and we unloaded our bikes. The apartment's owner helped us place them in the backyard, the domain of a testy dog who didn't seem happy to be sharing his home. He barked at us constantly while we parked our bikes.

After a quick shower, we headed out to walk the town. Sarria is the most popular starting point on the Camino Francés—it's just over 100 km (62 miles) from Santiago, the minimum distance required to earn the Compostela certificate. About two-thirds of the pilgrims on French Way start here, as it can be hiked in less than a week. The town was buzzing with people with eager smiles, fresh legs, and blister-free feet.

Marty and I strolled up the main street, found a tapas restaurant, and sat down. We had a wonderful dinner, including croquettas, tomatoes with Galician cheese, and local scallops served on open shells. I took a shell with me to replace the one I'd lost in the meseta.

Sitting at the table next to us was a group of five women in their fifties engaged in a lively conversation. We introduced ourselves. They were all from the U.K. and called themselves the "Camino Gals." They get together every year to walk a section of the Camino—they'd started with the section in the Pyrenees eight years before. This was their final year, and they were tackling the section from Sarria to Santiago. They spotted Marty's "Get Up and Ride" shirt.

"What is 'Get Up and Ride?'" asked Rachael, a tall, blonde woman who looked a bit like Rebecca from "Ted Lasso."

We told them our story—about our 40-year friendship, our bike trips together, and our book.

"So, I get it. Marty here is the fun guy—he just 'gets up and rides.' And Jim is the planner, right?"

"Pretty much," I said, laughing.

"We have a 'Jim' too," said Rachael. They all pointed to Clare, sitting at the other end of the table. She nodded, shrugged her shoulders and smiled.

"Spreadsheets?" Marty asked. Clare nodded.

"Are you staying in albergues? Or hotels?" I asked.

"Well, the first few trips, we stayed in albergues. Some great memories in those places alright. But now we stay in hotels. We're starting tomorrow."

"Carrying your backpacks or shuttling them?" Marty asked.

They looked at us as if we were crazy. "Are you kidding? We don't even *have* backpacks—we have huge rolling suitcases and use a luggage transfer service. Can't carry hair dryers and makeup cases on your back, you know."

The Camino Gals shared some great stories of their past trips, and we told them what it was like to experience the trail on a bicycle. We then paid our bill, got our passport stamps, said goodbye, and went back to our room, chatting as we walked.

"Jumbo, did that woman—Rachael—remind you of Rebecca from 'Ted Lasso?'"

"I was thinking the same thing! That's wild."

"What a cool tradition they have of doing a section every year," said Marty.

Prior to the trip, Marty and I had assumed that most people on the Camino would be doing the entire journey from St. Jean Pied de Port all at once. By now, we'd met many people, especially Europeans, who do parts of the Camino at different times. And we were about to meet a lot more who were starting in Sarria.

35

NOCTURNAL KNOWLEDGE
SARRIA TO ARZUA

Back in our room, I climbed into bed. Just as I was drifting off, the dog in the backyard began barking. After about half an hour, he stopped and I fell asleep. Ten minutes later, he cranked it up again. This time he barked for an hour nonstop. *How long can he keep this up?* Then, he took a break, only to continue yapping 30 minutes later. I tried using my earplugs to no avail. The pattern repeated itself for the next eight hours.

Finally, after a full night of torture, I got out of bed. We needed to have our bags packed and downstairs for the luggage shuttle by 7:15 a.m. It was pitch dark outside.

"Marty, did you sleep at all with that dog going all night?"

"Off and on. It was brutal."

I packed the espresso machine with coffee, filled it with water, and put it on the stove. Five minutes later, the black gold was ready to drink. And did we ever need it today.

"Jumbo, how much do you know about the Big Bang?" Marty asked as he packed his panniers and took the first sip of his coffee. This was an odd question at any time, but this early in the morning—in Spain—it was completely out of left field. However, Marty doesn't think like normal humans, so I went with it.

"Uh... not too much, really," I answered.

"You know about the James Webb telescope, right?"

"I've heard of it. Isn't it out West somewhere?"

"No, it's in space. Last year astronomers used it to discover a galaxy cluster called El Gordo that was formed six billion years after the big bang. And they keep discovering other galaxies that existed even closer to the big bang. Right now they're observing the Orion Nebula."

I was speechless. How was Marty able to sound so coherent, about a topic so complex, on no sleep and before coffee?

"How do you know all this?"

"Last night, when that dog kept barking, I was in and out of sleep, so I put in my AirPods. I sometimes listen to podcasts to help me fall asleep. It works—I'm usually out within ten minutes, and the podcast keeps rolling. I guess I'm learning things while I'm asleep. I'm multi-tasking, Jumbo." Marty was beaming.

"Wow," I said drowsily. "So, let me get this straight, Marty. You can't remember relatively simple things you hear while you're awake. But you have full recall of highly complex things you hear *while you're asleep*?"

"Yeah, weird, huh? I've been learning about the Webb telescope for months. The discoveries are fascinating."

"Good stuff, Marty. Now let's discover how we're gonna get our bags to Arzua."

We were downstairs with our bags by 7:00 a.m. Precisely at 7:15 a.m., a truck marked "Jacotrans" pulled up in the darkness.

"Buenos dias! Or... uh... noches?" said Marty. His Spanish was improving.

"Buenos dias," said the driver.

We handed him our bags. He looked at the tags we had filled out and shook his head.

"Portomarin," he said.

"Azzuria!" Marty said. "That's-o where-o they need-o to go!"

The Jacotrans guy looked confused.

"Azzurola!" Marty tried again, louder this time. Perhaps the increased volume would help him understand. He stared at us blankly.

"Arzua," I chimed in.

"Ahh," he said. He then shook his head and confirmed, "Portomarin. No Arzua." He was able to take our bags only as far as Portomarin, which was less than halfway to Arzua.

Understanding our predicament, he contacted another (competing) baggage service for us, and within fifteen minutes, a truck from NCS was there. The driver was yet another helpful Spaniard who was bright and cheery in the wee hours of this dark morning. He said he would take our bags to Arzua. We filled out the tags, loaded the bags on his truck, paid him, and watched as he drove off toward his next stop.

We had 71 miles to go to Santiago. Darkness was giving way to daylight, and it was 49 degrees and drizzling. Well, maybe it was 50, but 49 just sounds so much colder. What I do know is that I could see my breath, which is not a great thing when you're about to ride in the rain while creating your own windchill.

We were starting what would be a long and challenging ride—48 miles with 4,800 feet of total elevation gain. We put on our "waterproof" shells and took off at 8:30 a.m., the earliest start we'd had on the trip.

We saw a few pilgrims in rain gear heading out of town and followed them to the Camino. Immediately, we started climbing. And climbing. With our muscles working hard, we warmed up quickly.

Then came the descent. As our speed hit 30 mph, the wind

and rain blasted our faces and bodies. It felt like we were riding through a car wash inside a wind tunnel. I was shivering.

"Pinch yourself, Jumbo! Any idea where we are?"

"Spain!" I yelled out in the downpour. Even in the rain, it was simply beautiful.

An hour later, the rain eased up and turned into a gentle mist. We crossed a long, high bridge over the river Miño into the town of Portomarin. With its churches, archways, and cobblestone streets, Portomarin looked like most of the other medieval villages we'd seen. Except for one thing. It was built in the 1960s.

Portomarin started out life in the Middle Ages in a different spot—on the bank of the river Miño, in the valley below the bridge we'd just crossed. It thrived there for over 500 years until 1963, when the government decided to build a dam across the river to create a reservoir. Unfortunately, the engineers didn't anticipate where the water would collect, and the original town of Portomarin began to flood.

The government must have really wanted that reservoir. Instead of cutting the dam loose, they dismantled the historic buildings of the original village and rebuilt them, stone-by-stone and brick-by-brick, on higher ground. To make it look authentic, they added cobblestone streets as well as some houses and arcades. Voila, Portomarin 2.0 was born.

As rode into the "new town," Marty and I saw a remarkable stairway—rebuilt with stones from the old village—which led up to a chapel. We climbed to the top and were rewarded with a sweeping view of the river and valley below.

We rode underneath the stairway and through the town, stopping at the Iglesia de San Juan/San Nicolas, a 13th century fortress-style church that was re-built during the village's relocation. Looking closer, we could see numbers on the stones—reminders of the Great Portomarin Jigsaw Puzzle Project.

. . .

Reconstructed stairway to chapel in Portomarin

AFTER A QUICK PASSPORT STAMP, we returned to the Camino. By noon, the temperature reached the mid-60s and the sun came out. We were in a remote area. Looking to the right and left, the landscape was pure and unspoiled, with green forests stretched across the rolling mountains. No cars, no houses, no people.

But the Camino itself was packed. It seemed that all human life in the area was concentrated on this twenty-foot-wide pedestrian highway, heading in one direction, wearing backpacks. If you dropped in on this scene from Mars, hovering above it in your spacecraft, you might have thought these were refugees making a mass exodus from some humanitarian crisis. Or that a free ticket giveaway had just been announced to a Taylor Swift concert.

During our entire trip, when we approached pilgrims from behind, we'd adopted a habit of ringing our bells when we were about 25 yards away. Then, when we were just behind them, we'd say "Hola!" They would typically move to the side, and as we passed, we would offer a "Buen Camino." They would always reciprocate.

"Jumbo, how many times do you think we've said 'Buen Camino' on this trip?"

"Gotta be at least 200. Maybe 300."

"Yeah, probably even more. Do you think it's getting a little old? Like sort of rote by now? Do you think people really mean it? Or at this point are they just saying it?"

"I see what you mean…"

"I gotta believe everyone else is thinking the same thing by now. They just feel obliged to say it."

"Maybe we could come up with another expression to mix things up."

"Yeah, and maybe it would catch on," said Marty. "It would give people options. Who knows, maybe it would ultimately even replace the 'Buen Camino.'"

"Let's brainstorm. How about 'Keep Going?'" I offered.

"Get Up and Walk?"

"Press on, Pilgrim!"

We both thought for a bit, trying to come up with something better. I finally broke the silence.

"Well, 'Buen Camino' *has* been around for centuries, so it's gonna be kinda hard to replace. They probably vetted all kinds of other sayings and finally settled on it, like, 800 years ago. Plus, it's actually pretty good."

"Yeah, you're right," said Marty. "But maybe we should ration our 'Buen Caminos.' Like… how about this. What if we still go with the 'Hola' when we first see someone, but we wait for *them* to initiate the 'Buen Camino?' If they do, then we come back with *our* 'Buen Camino.'"

"Great idea. We're gonna need to save our 'Buen Caminos' for when we get to Santiago. There'll be a ton of people there."

As we pedaled, we tested out our novel approach. After a few tries, we agreed it seemed to work well.

. . .

A HALF HOUR LATER, we spotted a man ahead of us on a road bike, with large panniers on the back. As we approached from behind, we realized we knew this man.

It was Patrice from France, whom we hadn't seen since our first day on the Hill of Forgiveness.

"Bonjour Patrice!" I yelled.

He stopped and turned around. "Bonjour Jim! Bonjour Marty!"

"*Comment ça va?*" I asked him how he was, proudly trotting out one of the few French phrases I still remembered.

"*C'est très difficile!*" said Patrice. I nodded.

We rode together with him for a while. We wanted to know more about his trip and what he'd experienced. Sadly, due to the language barrier, we weren't able to have a conversation. After a couple of miles, he was ready for a break, and Marty and I wanted to continue. We said our farewells again.

Patrice! (near Portomarin)

As we made our way along the crowded Camino, we came upon a tiny church surrounded by a graveyard—the Iglesia de

Santiago de Lestedo. The heavy wooden doors were wide open, so we decided to stop and take a break.

Iglesia de Santiago de Lestedo

We were the only ones inside, except for the caretaker, an elderly man who stamped our passports. Along the left and right walls were several painted carvings—a Madonna, Jesus on the cross, and, of course, St. James the Moor Slayer. Marty and I took off our helmets and sat for a while, enjoying the solitude. Compared to the enormous cathedrals we'd toured earlier in the trip, it was nice to reflect in such an intimate place.

We stepped outside and chomped on some Peanut M&Ms. While we ate, I got a call from Pat, our cousin-in-law from Pittsburgh. He and his cousin, Dave, had been traveling in Portugal and Spain—we'd originally planned to meet them in Santiago de Compostela the next night when we arrived. They said they were actually fairly close to Arzua, so we agreed to meet them for dinner.

Just then, a dozen cyclists whizzed past us, riding identical bikes and wearing matching jerseys. We had seen very few cyclists on the trip thus far, and we'd never seen more than two people riding together. Were they a team of some sort? We got on our bikes and pedaled hard to catch up with them.

Cycling tour group: "El Camino en Bici"

It turned out they were on a tour from León to Santiago, led by an experienced guide who helped them navigate the route and identify points of interest. We introduced ourselves, and they invited us to ride with them for a while.

At Melide, we hit a "fork in the road." The original Camino went to the right and was the shorter path; a newer Camino trail went to the left and was constructed to allow pilgrims to avoid fording a stream. The cycling tour group went to the left, but Marty and I decided to take our chances and went the other way.

We rode through a wooded area, with a cool forest hugging the trail on both sides. It reminded us of riding in the mountains of western Pennsylvania. When we reached the stream, we saw pilgrims carefully stepping across a line of rocks. Some had stopped to soak their blister-ridden feet in the cool water. I took the cautious approach and walked my bike over the rocks. Marty took the direct route and rode right through the stream. You just can't take the kid out of this 65-year-old.

At around 5:00 p.m., we arrived at Arzua and found our

Airbnb. After showering, we met Pat and Dave at a restaurant. Pat's fluent Spanish was a big help, and it was great to spend time with friends from home after being away for so long. He treated us to a delicious meal with many local specialties. Marty and I said goodnight to Pat and Dave and went back to our apartment. The next day would be our last on the Camino.

Meeting Pat and Dave in Arzua

36

SANTIAGO DE COMPOSTELA

A canopy of eucalyptus trees arched overhead. Their blue-green leaves and peeling bark gave off a familiar smell—I think it was Campho-Phenique. Tiny streams of sunlight trickled through the thick foliage to the trail below. It was silent, except for the sound of gravel crunching under our tires. Our final hours on the Camino de Santiago.

We had planned what we thought would be a fairly easy day from Arzua to Santiago de Compostela—25 miles and 2,300 feet of climbing. But the entire Camino had been challenging, and each mile had been earned.

We got a late start after a leisurely morning, and the sun was already shining high in the cloudless, blue sky. It was the most perfect weather we'd had in the last two weeks—an ideal way to arrive in Santiago.

The Camino was really crowded. Large groups of school-children on day hikes were intermixed with pilgrims. Some had started a few days before in Sarria; others had begun five or six weeks earlier in France. The long-haulers were easy to spot—toned leg muscles, knee braces, and the telltale limp and stoop.

We hadn't met many Americans on the trail until now. On

this last stretch, the Camino was not only full of people from the U.S., we even met several from my childhood home in Northern Virginia.

Arnie and Eva, from Ashburn, VA, had started in France in mid-August and were still standing upright without injuries. Tom and Kelly, originally from Oregon and now also living in Ashburn, were on their second Camino in two years. Kelly described last year's experience as "magical." She said this year was good, but not quite the same. They weren't sure why— perhaps it was because the Camino had gotten a bit more touristy, or perhaps it was because "nothing is quite the same the second time you do it."

We had ten miles to go to Santiago. At that point, Marty finally gave the green light to talk about food.

"Hungry, Jumbo?"

"I could definitely eat."

"It's our last day. The M&Ms are great, but how about we sit down somewhere and have a beer and some lunch? Something other than paella?"

"Yeah, it would be great to get a burger."

"You think we could find wings?"

"I could destroy a Primanti sandwich right now." We both laughed. Primanti's is an iconic Pittsburgh eatery which serves sandwiches stacked with grilled meat, melted cheese, coleslaw, and French fries between two thick slices of Italian bread. Many people from outside the area think that's all we eat in Pittsburgh. It's not true. We also eat pierogies.

We spotted a trailside café with a sign outside showing pictures of six different types of pizzas. We sat down and ordered two of them, along with cervezas. The prices were noticeably higher than they'd been in the early stages—the businesses here were clearly benefiting from the increased traffic and wealthier demographic as we got closer to Santiago.

Before long, two exceedingly large pizzas were set in front of us. As we ate, we chatted.

"Jumbo, did you see the 'Wall of Wisdom' back there?"

"No, what was that?"

"You didn't see it? There was this wall along the side of the trail with a bunch of laminated sheets hung on it. Each one had a different saying or a philosophical question. Check this one out." Marty got out his phone and showed me a picture.

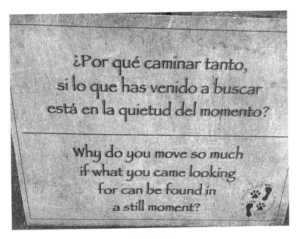

Wall of Wisdom

There it was, Marty's philosophy of life, encapsulated on a sheet of paper along the Camino. Unfortunately, I was moving too fast and missed it.

After lunch, our bellies distended, we got back on our bikes and immediately hit a huge climb. The Boston Marathon has "Heartbreak Hill," a grueling incline faced by runners at the twenty-mile mark. Marty and I named this one "Heartburn Hill." The pepperoni and tomatoes formed an acidic reaction unlike anything we'd experienced with Peanut M&Ms. To make matters worse, the beer had relaxed our muscles, which, of course, had assumed they were done for the day. But we needed them to kick in now and work some overtime. We ground our way to the top, rounded a corner, and were met with yet another hill. And then another.

Marty rode all the way up, but I had to dismount and walk. That's when I met Alina, who had started in France six weeks earlier. She was limping and wearing a knee brace.

Alina was from Germany and had made her first Camino four years before. She said the last few years had been difficult for her, and she felt she needed to do it again. Through this Camino, she'd been able to work through some of her challenges, grow in gratitude for all that she had, and was ready to return to the "real world" in a new frame of mind.

Alina

Next, we passed the town of O Pedrouzo, where most pilgrims get off the trail and stop for the day, allowing them to have a short walk into Santiago the next morning. Marty and I continued, with the trail nearly empty at this point. It was wonderful having such peace and quiet for the last few miles as we wound our way through the trees toward Santiago. I was pedaling just behind Marty, beginning to reflect on our experience the last two weeks.

Suddenly, I felt a "snap" under my left foot which yanked me out of my meditative state.

I looked down and saw the problem—my left pedal was broken. I'd used these same clipless pedals for many years with no problems, and they'd lasted the entire trip until now. "Clipless" is actually a bit of a misnomer, since one actually *does* clip one's shoes into these pedals. But it was an apt name at this point, since my pedal was now, in fact, missing a clip.

With just a few miles to go, I figured I could limp along with one working pedal. We pressed on and soon emerged from the woods and ascended a small knoll. We stopped at the top and gazed down to the valley below.

There it was—Santiago de Compostela. It looked like Oz in the distance—the somewhat mythical place we'd been thinking about and constantly moving towards over the last two weeks.

Later, we learned that this spot is known as the "Hill of Joy." I gotta say, they name these hills accurately in Spain. The Hill of Forgiveness was a beast. This one was pure jubilation.

And here's the best part—it was all downhill from here! Marty and I hopped on our bikes and coasted towards the city. During the descent, we met John and Janet from England who had walked the Camino Norte from Bilbao. All of the Camino routes converge here—the Portuguese, Inglés, Primitivo, Norte and Francés. These were the first people we'd met who had been on one of the other paths.

We rode through the outskirts of Santiago and then entered the historic district. Following the Camino markers along cobblestone streets and past medieval buildings, we generously dispatched all the "Buen Caminos" we'd been saving to every cheery pilgrim we passed. I felt like Scrooge at the end of *A Christmas Carol*.

"May as well give them out now," said Marty. "They won't do us any good back in Pittsburgh."

The city center was alive—people strolling around, sitting in cafés, some with backpacks, some without. We could feel the excitement in the air. Getting off our bikes, we walked them down the street, down a set of steps, and through a tunnel where a bagpiper was playing lively Celtic tunes.

We continued down another set of steps, rounded the corner to the left and saw...

The Cathedral of Santiago de Compostela.

Arriving at the Santiago de Compostela Cathedral

We had seen many pictures, but to be there in person was

beyond what we expected. The vast plaza was full of energy with pilgrims singing, talking, hugging, and crying. Perfect strangers were embracing each other. Some were drinking champagne. Some were lying down on their backpacks, barely able to stand. Some had indigestion from eating too much pizza for lunch.

We met people from all over the world who had come from multiple directions on different Camino paths. We saw pilgrims reuniting with their families who had made the trip to Santiago to greet them. Everyone was celebrating together and sharing their experiences.

Next to us was a group of a dozen women, all with matching shirts, who were singing a song in Spanish in unison. They invited us to join them in their revelry, and we did, although we knew neither the tune nor the lyrics.

It's hard to describe how it felt as we soaked in the moment with thousands of others in the plaza. It was a combination of relief and joy, along with a tinge of sadness knowing that our Camino had ended.

A few minutes later, Pat and Dave arrived and shared in our celebration. Pat had previously walked the Camino Portuguese, so he knew his way around town. He led us over to the Pilgrim's Reception Office to get our Compostela certificates.

The building was a bustling place. A screen on the wall displayed a real-time count of the number of pilgrims who had arrived that day. At around 5:00 p.m., it registered 2,200. We saw the statistics of total pilgrims year-to-date: it was over 350,000, on pace for a record year. Right now, as you read this, five more pilgrims just received their certificates in Santiago.

We answered some questions on a computer indicating the Camino sections we'd ridden, then showed the attendant our Pilgrim Passports. Cyclists need to ride at least 200 km (125 mi) in order to qualify for the Compostela certificate. We had ridden a total of 440 km (275 mi), but it hadn't been contiguous, and we weren't sure if we would qualify. Happily, we were given our certificates, written in Latin, with our Latin names on them —"Jacobum" for me, "Martinum" for Marty.

Compostela certificate

With our paperwork in hand, we exited the Pilgrim Office and saw a familiar face. It wasn't Pat or Dave. It was Patrice.

"Bonjour, Patrice!"

"Bonjour, Jim! Bonjour, Marty!"

"*Ça va?*" I asked how he was doing.

"*Oui! C'est fini! C'était super!*" (Yes! It's finished! It was super!)

We had many questions we wanted to ask him—what towns he had stayed in, what he'd thought of the experience, and most importantly, how he'd managed to arrive in Santiago at the same time as us, given we'd taken a bus and two taxis! But the language barrier made it too difficult, and all we could manage was a "high five" and a celebratory photo.

We said goodbye to Patrice and headed to our Airbnb, a few steps away from the church. Marty and I unloaded our panniers for the last time, then showered and changed.

Celebrating with Patrice in Santiago de Compostela

The front door of the building was unlocked, and the security of the place seemed a little sketchy. Since there was a safe in the bathroom, we decided we'd use it.

"I'll program it, Jumbo. What combination should we use? We need four digits."

I paused briefly. "How about the Pittsburgh area code—412 —and then a "1" at the end?"

"Perfect."

I handed Marty my passport and wallet, taking out some cash and a credit card to use for the next couple of days. He went into the bathroom and reappeared a few minutes later.

"All set?" I asked.

"Yup, all good. Hey, how about we celebrate with an ice cream?"

We had been wanting ice cream the entire trip but hadn't been able to find it at the right time. Thinking it would help soothe our heartburn, we figured now was the time. We found a gelato shop, ordered two cups, and took our first spoonfuls. Marty looked over at me, watching my facial expression.

"Don't say anything Jumbo. Just keep quiet."

"Why?"

"I'm really enjoying this. If it's not good, just keep it to your-self." Marty was chuckling.

I laughed and ate my gelato in silence.

(Pssst—it was fantastic.)

37

BARNACLES
SANTIAGO DE COMPOSTELA

As evening approached, we decided it was time to really celebrate. Pat called to let us know that he and Dave had confirmed a dinner reservation. We walked over to the place and met them there.

It wasn't just any eatery—it was a Michelin-rated restaurant with a fifteen-course prix-fix meal. Marty and I had no business being there in our shorts and cleated bike shoes. But they seemed willing to serve us anyway and led us to our table.

In a strong Spanish accent, the waitress gave an overview of the dining experience we were about to have. We understood some of it, but we were so famished that we just wanted to get things started.

She then gave a romantic description of the first course, which we didn't understand at all. She also explained that they would be pairing each course with a local Galician wine.

The first course came. I looked down at my plate. In the center was a small stick with five droplets—each one a different color—evenly spaced down its length. We were advised not to eat the stick.

Droplets for dinner?

About fifteen minutes later, the second course arrived. A small sphere about the size of a golf ball sat in a wooden bowl alongside a tiny seafood sculpture on a wooden pedestal. The waitress began explaining what they were in broken English, but before she could finish, we had already wolfed them down.

Another fifteen minutes passed before the third course. We thought the waitress said "barnacle" when describing it, but that couldn't have been right. Maybe we heard her wrong. Or maybe "barnacle" was actually a Spanish word for something entirely different, like a shrimp or a mussel. Similar to that whole "tortilla" thing.

We asked her to clarify. She struggled a bit, then reached into her pocket, pulled out her phone, typed something into Google, and showed us the search result:

Yep, we were getting barnacles.

They came in a teacup—three crustaceans for each of us, along with some seaweed and salty broth. We looked at each other. Should we eat these rubbery creatures scraped from the bottom of some unknown ship? I was so hungry that I swallowed the entire contents in one gulp.

Marty with barnacles in teacup

I did some quick math. Fifteen courses, fifteen minutes apart, with about fifteen calories per course. At this rate, we'd be here for over three hours with a total of less than 250 calories. We had just burned over 3,000 calories on the day's ride, and the pizza and gelato were a distant memory. My body was starting to consume itself. We needed a new game plan.

Just then, a woman approached our table with a bread basket.

"Raisin bread or white bread?" she offered.

"YES!!" Marty and I said simultaneously. She gave each of us two big hunks, and we plowed them down quickly. Nothing had ever tasted so good (no offense, barnacles).

We saw her go by again.

"Uno more, por favor?" Marty asked, using all of the Spanish he'd picked up over the last two weeks. "Raisin?"

She promptly laid another generous piece of raisin bread on each of our bread plates. We devoured them instantly.

"I'm surprised we're not getting a wine pairing with our

raisin bread course," I whispered to Marty. "This seems to be the bulk of our meal tonight."

"Yeah," Marty joked. "What would you pair with a September 2023 raisin bread? A Galician white?"

At this point, we sensed that the staff was getting nervous. The bread basket was nearly empty, and many other tables in the restaurant hadn't yet been offered any.

"Jumbo, I'll bet they're back there in the kitchen right now freaking out."

"Yeah, the owner's probably yelling, 'why'd you serve those two guys all the bread? They're dressed like slobs!' And the waitress is saying, 'they may ask for even more—what do we do?'"

Marty snickered. "Right, and the owner's telling her, 'Try to slow them down. Don't go near their table with the bread basket. And quickly fire up the oven and bake more!'"

Our speculation was confirmed. We stopped being offered bread, and three courses later, a small scallop was served with a razor-thin slice of raisin bread. They were rationing.

The dinner did, in fact, last three hours, and it was fantastic. By the end, the courses actually got a bit bigger, and by the third dessert course, I wished I hadn't eaten so much raisin bread.

We made a joke that it would be great to take some raisin bread home with us. Pat immediately got up and talked to the waitress. The second baking round must have been complete at that point: at the end of our meal, our waitress presented us with a take-out bag with a full loaf inside.

Marty and I said goodnight to Pat and Dave and headed back to our room. Tomorrow would be our last full day in Spain.

38

LAND'S END

SANTIAGO DE COMPOSTELA AND CAPE FINISTERRE

I woke up early and looked out the window to see the sun just coming up. Marty was still sleeping. I let him rest while I got dressed, stepped outside, and walked back to the cathedral. The plaza was nearly empty—it had a completely different vibe compared to the lively party scene the day before.

I met a family from Mexico who had hiked the Camino Primitivo together. The parents had been in Santiago 34 years before on their honeymoon—this time they brought their adult children and made the pilgrimage together. They said they were headed to visit the tomb of St. James and invited me to join them.

We walked over to the cathedral's side door together. It was just opening, and we were the second group to enter. We passed through a short hallway and saw the tomb, in an alcove set back behind iron bars. Then we saw the tombs of St. James' two disciples, Athanasius and Theodore, which were also discovered here in the ninth century.

Tomb of St. James

The walkway led us to a narrow staircase behind the main altar. At the top of the steps, we found ourselves looking at the back of the bust of St. James, which was facing the sanctuary. The tradition is for pilgrims to embrace St. James from behind —I followed the other pilgrims and took my turn. In the silence of the nearly empty 800-year-old cathedral, it was moving for me to have a moment alone with my patron saint.

Afterwards, I walked around inside the church. The interior was not as vast as the cathedrals we'd visited in Burgos and León. In fact, for a world-renowned cathedral with such a grand façade, it struck me as somewhat small and intimate. But it was overflowing with ornate detail.

The pillars near the altar were painted blue, with scallop shells and other ornamentation related to St. James. The main altarpiece was stunning. Made of gold and silver, it surrounded the entire altar area from floor to ceiling, with a golden canopy above. Every inch was decorated—there were sculptures of at least a dozen angels and other figures, pillars wrapped in gold, and three likenesses of St. James, one above the other. The bust I had just embraced was at the bottom, now visible from the front. Above that was St. James the Pilgrim with his two disciples. And at the very top was St. James the Moor Slayer, complete with unhappy Moors underneath.

Main altar in Cathedral of Santiago de Compostela

Hanging from the ceiling in front of the altar was the famous *Botafumeiro*—the huge incense burner which has swung through the church on ropes since the Middle Ages as a way of masking the smell of sweaty pilgrims who hadn't bathed in over a month. I remembered seeing it in action in "The Way."

Today it is swung only on Holy Days (e.g. Christmas and Easter) and when VIPs are present at Mass.

After visiting some of the side chapels, I exited the cathedral and walked back to the plaza in front of the church. It was just after 8:00 a.m.—I had the place mostly to myself and sat down with some time to reflect.

It was over. It had been an incredible adventure with Marty and a memorable trip of a lifetime. Had it been "magical" or "life-changing?" If I was honest with myself, the answer was "no." I'd be returning essentially as the same "Jumbo" I was two weeks earlier. No "new me 2.0."

But in small ways, there were changes. I had lost seven pounds, and Marty had lost ten.

Even more importantly, spending time with Marty on the Camino helped me realize that it's okay when things don't go according to plan. Our Camino hadn't unfolded exactly as I'd envisioned, but it was in the mishaps and challenges that we experienced the best part of the Camino—the unconditional willingness of people to help each other.

The trip had also given me time to reflect and pray in some of the most beautiful cathedrals in Spain, as well as in intimate, small churches in tiny Camino villages. I would need more time to fully process the experience, but as I sat in front of the cathedral, I felt it was the perfect way for me to transition into retirement—and grandfatherhood.

I made my way back to our apartment and found Marty, who was just waking up. We munched on the leftover raisin bread as we drank our coffee and discussed the plan for the day. We agreed we would meet Pat and Dave at the Pilgrim's Mass at noon at the cathedral, then visit Cape Finisterre in the afternoon.

But first we had work to do—we had to get boxes for our bikes and pack them up. We went to the post office (Correos) and bought boxes and tape. Then we dismantled our bikes and packed them inside, storing them in the basement of our building.

With that task completed, we headed to the cathedral for Mass. Knowing it would be crowded, we arrived an hour early. There was already a long line—Pat and Dave joined us at the back, and we inched slowly toward the building. As the clock struck noon, we had finally made it to the entrance, with a huge column of people still behind us.

Just as we reached the doorway, the guards told us Mass was starting, and the church was full. We were disappointed, but we decided to wait for a bit. Sure enough, a minute later they motioned to us and said they had standing room for a few more people. We were the last to enter.

Now packed with people, the cathedral had been transformed from the quiet, empty place I'd experienced just a few hours earlier. Mass was in Spanish, so we didn't understand much. Since it wasn't a Holy Day, I didn't expect to see the Botafumeiro in use, and as the Mass was ending, it still hadn't moved from its stationary position.

The Botafumeiro

Then, to my surprise, during the closing hymn, six men in

red cloaks got up and began pulling on ropes in perfect synchrony. They sent the smoking Botafumeiro soaring through the air, swinging like a pendulum from one nave to the other. Either there were some VIPs in the house, or they were sending a message to Marty and me that we needed a bath.

AFTER MASS, Pat and Dave drove us to the coast at Cape Finisterre, the end of the original pagan and Roman route which preceded the Camino in ancient times. About one in ten pilgrims today travel the additional 50 miles to come here. Hoping we'd find a place for a picnic, we stopped and bought ham, chorizo, cheese, bread, and champagne.

It was windy and foggy when we pulled into the parking lot. As we stood on the headlands, we saw only open ocean on both sides. Waves smashed against the jagged rocks below, marking the end of their journey across the Atlantic. A large cross sat at the edge of a high cliff, indicating the "unofficial" end of the Camino. A single road ran the length of the peninsula, passing a hotel and ending at the Fisterra Lighthouse, which has stood watch over this scene since 1853.

This is the place where Edward, the e-biker whom we'd met on our second day in Estella, planned to sprinkle his wife's ashes in the ocean. It's also near Muxia, where Martin Sheen's character in "The Way" spreads the last of his son's ashes.

Cape Finisterre is known to locals as *Costa da Morte*, or "Coast of Death." It's notorious for its wicked storms, thick fog, aggressive currents, and unforgiving rocky outcrops. If you drained all the water from around the cape, you would see the skeletons of nearly 1,000 ships strewn about the bottom. In fact, 25 ships sunk here in a single night on October 28, 1596. And one of Spain's worst ecological disasters occurred here in November 2002, when an oil tanker was caught in a storm and sank a week later.

People have died swimming here, too. In September 2019, an Irish pilgrim went for a dip at sunset and was quickly caught in the strong currents. His friends recovered him from the ocean but were unable to revive him. And ten years earlier, a pilgrim from Poland climbed down to the rocks to take some photos. He was swept into the sea, and it took multiple boats and helicopters three days to locate his body.

It's hard to imagine that someone could walk 500 miles, climb 30,000 feet, and survive over a month of rainstorms, sun and heat exposure, blisters, ankle injuries, and albergue-induced insomnia, only to perish on the last day just before boarding the flight home.

Luckily, as you've surmised based on the existence of this book, that didn't happen to us. We found an area with large boulders where we could sit and look out at the ocean, away from the crowds. We had a picnic celebration on the cliffs together with Pat and Dave, ending with the Cohiba cigars gifted to Marty by the criminal who stole his credit card. The pagans should have been so fortunate.

Cape Finisterre

39

RE-ENTRY

After Finisterre, we headed back to Santiago, with Dave as our designated driver. During our fifteen-course dinner the previous night, Pat had spoken with the owner who said she had another restaurant in Santiago which claimed to have "the best hamburgers in all of Spain." We were ready for a burger, so Pat called the owner from the car and asked her (in Spanish) about the place. He paused mid-conversation and covered the mouthpiece.

"Hey guys," Pat said. "She's now saying it's *not* actually the *best* burger in Spain. It's the *third best*. You still wanna go?"

"*What?*" I exclaimed, looking at Marty. "The country's best burger just got downgraded two notches—*overnight*?"

Marty spoke up. "At this rate, by the time we get there, it'll be down to fourth or fifth! Hurry up!" Dave stepped on the gas.

We arrived at the restaurant. Right there on the menu, it stated: "The Japan Burger—Third Best Hamburger in Spain." We ordered four of them.

"How do you think they determine the ranking?" Marty asked as we waited for our food. "Do you think there is some sort of country-wide competition?"

"I'm guessing they just claim it," said Pat. "It's all marketing."

"Actually, claiming third sounds more believable, doesn't it?" I said. "If they said 'best burger,' no one would believe it. 'Third best' sounds more legit, like there was some sort of expert ranking involved, right?"

"Jumbo, how many burgers have we seen on the menus in Spain over the last two weeks? None! 'Third best' might actually be last place."

The burgers arrived, and they were excellent. They were indeed the best (and only) burgers we'd had in Spain.

Marty and I said goodbye to Pat and Dave, then walked back to our apartment and went to bed. The bell from the cathedral and the partying outside kept us up most of the night, but it didn't matter. There would be plenty of time to sleep when we got back to Pittsburgh.

THE NEXT MORNING, we were up very early. I called a taxi-van to come pick us up and take us to the airport. Then, I walked over to the safe to retrieve our passports and wallets. I punched in the combination. Nothing happened.

I tried it again. Nada.

"Marty, did you program this with the code we agreed on?"

"Yeah, I'm pretty sure I did."

"I can't get it to work."

"I don't know, Jumbo. It's possible I could have keyed it in wrong. It was a lot to remember. Plus, I didn't have my reading glasses."

I sighed. *It was four digits. The taxi is on its way. We can't miss this flight.* I took a deep breath, trying to practice what I'd learned on the Camino. *It's okay when things go wrong. It's okay.*

In my pre-caffeinated fog, I wracked my brain and tried to think of all the ways Marty could have entered "4-1-2-1."

He probably just forgot and put the extra "1" at the beginning instead of at the end. I tried "1-4-1-2." Swing-and-a-miss.

He's nearly blind without his glasses. He once typed "Jumbo" instead of "Jimbo." I looked at the keypad. Could he have mistaken the "2" for a "7?" I tried "4-1-7-1." Whiff #2.

I didn't know how many strikes I'd get before the thing shut down. This next guess had better be good. I thought for a few moments. *What Would Marty Do?*

What if he did both? Could he have forgotten to put the "1" at the end <u>and</u> mis-typed the "2"?

I carefully typed in "1-4-1-7." Click. Bingo. Home run.

I now know Marty better than anyone else on the planet. Sorry, Belle.

I quickly emptied the safe. We packed up our things and stepped outside just as the taxi was arriving in the darkness. The driver helped us load our boxes in the back, then drove us to Santiago Airport.

When we arrived, we checked our bikes as luggage, as we had done on the flight from Pittsburgh two weeks before. I asked the attendant if we needed to do anything special to make sure the bikes made it through all three legs on two different airlines to the U.S.

"Not to worry, your luggage follows you," she replied. *Where had I heard this before?*

Our first flight from Santiago to Madrid was uneventful. When we landed, I checked my "Find My" app. The bikes had indeed followed us. At this point, we were far less concerned about them than we were on our way over to Spain. I needed a break from my old friend (the bike, that is) for a while, anyway.

We had one more connection through London and then the long flight back to Pittsburgh. We landed at Heathrow and made our way to the British Airways gate for our transatlantic flight. As we boarded an elevator, we noticed a woman wearing a ball cap, accompanied by a personal escort.

"Marty, does she look familiar to you?" I whispered. I was pretty sure I knew who she was, but I wanted Marty to confirm.

Marty tried not to stare while stealing a few glances at the woman just a few feet away.

"Maybe," he said under his breath.

We then boarded a tram to the next terminal. The same woman was there, along with her assistant. I took another glance. This time I was sure. I looked at Marty and he nodded.

She was none other than Hannah Waddingham (a.k.a. Rebecca from "Ted Lasso"). Having met her lookalike in Sarria, we were now sharing a train car with the real thing. She saw my "Get Up and Ride" shirt and smiled. I took that as an indication that she'd read the book and had clearly enjoyed it.

We arrived at the British Airways gate, and I opened my "Find My" app to check on the bikes.

Foiled again. They were still in Madrid.

I told Marty—we shook our heads in disbelief and laughed.

"What happened to 'your luggage follows you?'" he asked.

"I guess that may generally be true, except when your luggage gets a little tired and decides to take a rest in Madrid. Which seems to happen a lot."

We asked the British Airways gate attendant what we should do. Somehow everything sounds so much more positive with a British accent. As I recall, she said something like this:

"We're terribly sorry, gents, your bicycles are indeed in Madrid. But you'll receive them forthwith, or at least within a fortnight or two, and they'll likely be in little bits and pieces and what not. But not to worry, lads, whilst they may be lost for now, we're keen to find them, and we do hope you have a jolly good time on your flight home."

Our disappointment quickly faded when we learned we had been upgraded to business class on the flight to Pittsburgh.

It was a residual benefit of the "old me" flying over 100,000 miles per year while Marty was "chillin" in the 'burgh.

It was an odd configuration—our seats faced each other—which, of course, added to the hilarity of the 7.5-hour flight. Marty enjoyed playing with the various seat reclining options while struggling with all the choices on the menu. He also required a bit of education on what to do with the wet towel.

Marty in business class

Marty also kept his "streak" intact. This one really tested him, as he consumed every beverage offered during the entire flight—pre-takeoff champagne, sparkling water and wine with dinner, and port wine with dessert. I tempted him: I told Marty that if he was ever going to use an airplane bathroom, this was his chance, as it was quite large and squeaky clean. I even went into the bathroom and took a video of the interior, complete with narration, so Marty would understand that he had nothing to fear behind that small door (I received a distinct look of disapproval from the woman waiting in line as I exited). But Marty resisted and stayed true to his mission.

We landed in Pittsburgh and received a royal reception from Katie and Belle, complete with balloons, posters and "Buen Caminos." We didn't need to wait for any luggage, one upside to our bikes still being in Madrid. We headed straight home.

A hero's welcome from Katie and Belle at Pittsburgh Airport

It took Marty and me several days to decompress and recover from jet lag. Two days after we arrived home, I sat down on our sofa in the afternoon and fell asleep. I woke up an hour later, completely disoriented, and thought I was still in Spain. I looked out the window saw a mangled bike box sitting outside the front door. What was our house doing in Spain? Why is that box sitting there? Where is Marty? Then I gradually "came to" and realized where I was.

I went outside and checked out the box, which had been left by a courier. It looked like it had been through a hurricane. But aside from some scrapes and gouges, the bicycle itself was fine, and nothing was missing. My luggage had followed me after all; it had just taken its time.

After I pulled the bike out of the box, I realized it was still encrusted in Spanish mud. I hesitated a bit, but eventually hosed it down, washing away some of the memory of the trip.

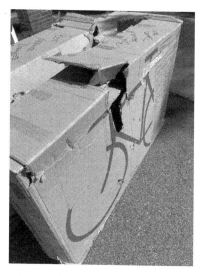

Remains of our bike boxes upon arrival in Pittsburgh

40

REFLECTIONS

As each day passed, the trip felt more and more like a dream. Did it actually happen?

For the first couple of days, I caught myself greeting people with "Hola" and thanking them with "Gracias." We'd repeated these words over and over during our two weeks in Spain, and they were engrained in my brain. But as the days passed, even these expressions faded to English.

I became much more tuned in to Camino-related things after returning from Spain. The following weekend, our granddaughter was christened. A metal scallop shell was used by the deacon to scoop water from the baptismal font and send a trickle down her tiny head, eliciting a brief shriek and a few tears before she settled back down and fell asleep. The deacon explained that the scallop shell used in Christian baptism is a symbol which reflects back to St. James and the Camino. Baptism is the start of a person's "pilgrimage" to heaven, and the scallop shell symbolizes that pilgrimage.

Scallop shell used at our granddaughter's baptism

A week after returning, while driving on a road I'd been on many times, I stopped at an intersection. Looking up, I noticed the street sign—"Santiago Road." I'd seen it in the past, but it had never registered with me before. And as I was walking in my neighborhood the next day, I looked down at the sidewalk. The power company had marked it with a yellow arrow. Was it a buried cable, or were they pointing the way to Santiago?

Reminders of the Camino in Pittsburgh

After our return, many people asked us "How was the trip?" It's impossible to answer that question in a few words.

"Awesome." "Incredible." "Amazing." "Unbelievable." "Exhausting."

The trip was all of those things, to be sure. But it was more. Here, I'll share some reflections along with some practical take-aways. These may be helpful if you or someone you know is considering a Camino cycling pilgrimage.

Our adventure had highs and lows, as every Camino pilgrim experiences. The trip was physically challenging and mentally draining for me. I had spent a lot of time choosing the places to stay and determining how far I thought we could ride each day based on the elevation gains between towns. I booked Airbnbs and hotels in advance.

On the positive side, we had very nice accommodations in the center of each town, at a reasonable price. The downside was that we had a set schedule and a place we needed to be each night. When bad weather, body aches, and equipment issues occurred, it was difficult to adjust.

If we returned to the Camino, we would primarily stay in private rooms (with private baths) in the albergues, which were going for around 30 to 50 euros per night for two people. This would also have given us more opportunity to interact with other pilgrims. These rooms can be booked in advance, but we'd probably book them the day before once we knew where we'd likely end up the next day.

We would also stay in some of the tiny villages. Now that we've seen the bigger cities—Logroño, Burgos, León—it would be good to experience the quietness of the small towns we passed through quickly during the day. For a first-time Camino pilgrim, the larger cities are indeed beautiful and there is a lot to see. It's a good idea to plan to spend two days in Pamplona, Burgos, and León if you can afford the time. This also gives your body time to rest and recover before the next leg.

If we did the Camino again, we would also plan to ride fewer miles per day. Marty and I typically have no trouble riding 60 to 80 miles on rail trails. For our Camino, I had planned for an average of about 40 miles a day, with some days as short as 25 to 35 miles and others as long as 60 miles. The long days were far too long, given the climbing (nearly 20,000 total feet for us), the weight of our bags, and the rough condition of the trail. We had trained extensively for this trip, including riding a lot of hills, yet it was still very taxing. It would be better to shoot for 25 to 30 miles each day. This would give enough time to enjoy a more leisurely morning, stop for lunch, and have time in the afternoon to chat with pilgrims and see the town.

Most walking pilgrims are on the trail by 6:00 to 8:00 a.m. and arrive in the next town by around 2:00 to 3:00 p.m. They are sitting in the cafés in the afternoon, drinking wine, nursing blisters, and sharing stories (not slugging it out on the meseta like us). This is a great time to connect with others. Also, most of the churches, monasteries, and museums in Spain close from 2:00 to 4:30 p.m., so this is a good time to arrive, shower, do laundry, and get settled in. Restaurants don't serve dinner until 7:00 p.m. or later, so we often needed to snack at a bar beforehand to make it until dinner.

Many sections of the Camino prior to the town of Sarria are not well marked, so it's easy to lose the trail, especially when you're moving at a faster pace on a bike. And some sections are not really rideable at all.

Essentially, the Camino is a walking trail and is made for walking. Bikers can ride it, but it's tough, and we had to ride around many walkers. We did in a respectful way—taking it slow, ringing our bells, and being generous with our "Holas," "Graciases," and "Buen Caminos." But we ended up getting on the roads a lot, following bike routes on Google Maps. Google often took us away from the Camino, sometimes putting us on dirt paths or leading us to bridges or roads that were closed because of construction. We spoke with other cyclists who had downloaded tried-and-true bike routes (GPS tracks) on their Garmins. We would do that next time, or more closely follow the road route maps in Mike Wells' "Cycling the Camino" book.

A key discovery for us was finding that the luggage transfer services used by walkers to shuttle backpacks can also be used by cyclists to shuttle panniers. For twelve to eighteen euros, these services (Jacotrans or NCS) shuttle two saddlebags as far as 45 miles. They make their rounds in the mornings (typically before 8:00 a.m.) and deliver the bags at your destination by around 2:00 to 3:00 p.m. We started doing this out of necessity once Marty's rack broke, but we wished we'd done it from the start. Both Jacotrans and NCS have envelopes in many of the hotels and albergues. You put the money in the envelope, fill out the destination address, and tie the envelope onto your bag. You can also make a reservation on their websites. Using Apple AirTags in our panniers (and on our bikes) enabled us to know where they were at any point.

Even with the benefit of shuttling the bags, it's not easy living out of panniers for two weeks. It took us a long time each morning to re-pack our bags so we could fit everything and stay organized. We got better at it as the trip went on. We kept everything in categorized Ziploc bags so we could squeeze the air out. And we tried to pack the things we needed each day into one pannier so we didn't need to open up the other bag every night.

Regarding the bicycles themselves, we used hardtail mountain bikes. Without question, these were the right bikes for the Camino. The wide, knobby tires and front suspension were essential for many parts of the journey. These bikes also provided a more comfortable ride with better control versus a gravel bike with drop handlebars.

At home, I mainly ride rail trails, and our past GAP/C&O trips had been on flat, relatively smooth paths. In fact, on those trips (and in the first "Get Up and Ride" book), the trail was almost a non-entity and barely factored into the ride or the story. On the Camino, however, the cycling was a tremendous challenge, which is why the trail itself became a major "character" in this book!

We were fortunate in that we had no flat tires and no major mechanical issues (other than Marty's rack and my pedal). There are bike shops in most of the large and mid-sized cities, and we found pumps sitting outside most of them. This allowed us to top off our tires in the morning before heading out, even if the shops hadn't yet opened.

In terms of gear, we had rain shells which ended up soaking through—not really what a rain shell is intended to do, Next time I'll invest in a high-quality rain jacket and waterproof covers for my riding shoes. We saw other cyclists with these, and their feet stayed dry while mine were soaked through. The Ortlieb panniers we'd bought (gravel packs) worked well and kept everything dry inside.

In terms of technology, having a phone mount on my handlebars (with an OtterBox Lifeproof case) was essential. My headlight doubled as a phone charger, which I used every day. We also bought a travel wi-fi device at Madrid Airport and a cheap 30-day data plan. Both Marty and I used this as a mobile hotspot throughout the trip, so we didn't need to rely on our cell phone data.

Regarding food and water, there are places to get food fairly often along the way, and there are potable water fountains every few miles. The bars and cafés will also fill up your water bottles. We couldn't find energy bars in the grocery stores, but we did find some in the bike shops. And Peanut M&Ms are available everywhere!

If we did it again, we would also learn some Spanish. Adding an "o" to the ends of English words doesn't really cut it —most Spanish people in the small towns (and on the Camino) speak little to no English. Some speak French, so if you know French, you may get by. But we wished we had taken the time to learn some Spanish, as it would have made things easier when we ran into logistical challenges and when we wanted to order food. Also, the largest population on the Camino seemed to be people from Spain, so it would have also helped in interacting with fellow pilgrims.

Regarding flights, it's a good idea to schedule a couple of extra days in the "starting" city (Pamplona for us) before commencing the ride. Due to our transatlantic flight being delayed a full day, and the bikes not making it on our flight to Pamplona, we needed all the buffer time. If we hadn't set things up this way, we would have had to reschedule all our accommodations as we had planned just one night in each place.

We also learned there is no one way to do the Camino. Some walkers end up taking buses and taxis across certain sections. Others cycle parts of it and walk other parts. Some walk or ride a single section or do a different section each year. Marty and I ended up taking a bus and a couple of taxis. Aside from a few walkers joking with us that we were "cheating" by using bikes, there is no judgement placed by anyone on others on the Camino. Everyone is out there, in it together, and each person's experience is his or her own. And everyone celebrates together at the end in Santiago de Compostela.

If we repeated the Camino Francés, Marty and I agreed we would want to do a combination of walking and cycling. We might walk the section from St. Jean Pied de Port over the Pyrenees to Pamplona and continue walking to Burgos. Then we would rent bikes and ride the meseta from Burgos to León, and possibly continue riding to Astorga and even Villafranca del

Bierzo (this was some of the best cycling). At that point, we would probably turn in the bikes and walk the rest of the way.

Renting a bike would remove the hassle of flying them over to Spain, tracking them, and dealing with the boxes. There are several companies that rent quality bicycles (Bicigrinos, Camino Ways)—you just need to bring your own helmet.

There are other Camino routes, and we met people in Santiago who had been on the Camino Norte, Portuguese, and Primitivo. Those routes are less populated, which may make it easier for cyclists. However, we heard the Norte has much more climbing than the French Way (our route). One pilgrim who had walked all three routes told me that, given the amount of foot traffic on the French Way between Sarria and Santiago, he prefers the Norte or Portuguese. He said these other routes give more time to meditate on your own during the day, while still meeting up with pilgrims in the albergues at night.

While the scenery, sights, and food were memorable, the best part about the Camino is the people. We had many once-in-a-lifetime chance encounters with people from all over the world. And, in the case of Patrice, it ended up being three times.

Even though we couldn't really converse with Patrice, we communicated through the unspoken language of our shared experience. On our first day, at the Hill of Forgiveness, we commiserated as we walked our bikes over the loose rocks, trying not to twist an ankle. "C'est très difficile!" he said, smiling. Nine days later, near Portomarin, he had been through the same cold rain, wind, and hot sun that we had experienced, and he had climbed the same mountains we'd climbed. "C'est très difficile!" he said again, still smiling. Then, in Santiago de Compostela, no longer focused on how "difficile" the trip was, he was basking in the joy of having completed his journey.

We don't know what motivated Patrice to embark on the

Camino. Was it the cycling challenge? Losing a loved one? Trying to find his "place in the world?" Maybe he was wondering the same thing about us.

Watching people add their stones to the millions of others at the Iron Cross made me realize that even though we may be from different countries, speak different languages, and have different faith backgrounds and customs, we all share a few things in common. We all (hopefully) have some "peak" experiences in our lives, we all have some struggles and burdens, and we all need the support of a friend.

The Camino provides that. Many start alone, but no one ends alone. It felt like being part of a big family. None of the people we met cared about each other's politics, religion, or ethnic background. The Camino gives pilgrims time to reflect, converse, and build new friendships; sometimes places them in situations where they need to rely on each other; and sends them home with a better perspective on how to live.

Emilio Estevez (son of Martin Sheen and director of "The Way") said in an interview that he believes that if everyone would make this pilgrimage, it would "change our politics." I think he's right.

We were overwhelmed by the unconditional generosity and kind spirit of the Spanish people. We began calling them "Camino Angels." On three occasions in three different cities, locals offered to help us arrange a luggage transfer by placing a call for us. In Pamplona, our Airbnb host felt so badly about our bikes being lost that he took it upon himself to drive to the airport to locate them. Outside of Los Arcos, when I lost Marty, a stranger helped me find him. In Carrión de Los Condes, the hotel owner set up a clothes-drying rack for us and laid out our garments, sock by sock.

And the best of all: the man who opened up the back of his van at a gas station after we'd spent nine brutal hours riding on the meseta. He saw our situation and, without hesitating or even asking where were going, put our filthy bikes in the back of his pristine van and drove us to our destination. He had no idea how much he did for us that day. If it wasn't for him, we might still be out there.

It was a Buen Camino. And it will be in our memories forever (until Marty forgets).

EPILOGUE

"Lie still," said the nurse.

I was on my back on the table, trying not to move.

"Okay, lift your legs up on this box and lie still again."

She pushed a few buttons, and several minutes later, the DXA scan was over.

It was December 2023, three months after we'd returned from the Camino. I remembered my chiropractor mentioning that he'd seen some loss of bone mass during my first appointment in April, so I thought I would follow up with the scan as he'd suggested. I didn't expect much would come of it.

A few days later, I got a call from my doctor.

"Mr. Shea, I have some bad news."

"What?" I sat down, bracing myself.

"Your scan shows you have severe osteoporosis. It's particularly severe in your spine."

"How? What does that mean? How... is that possible?"

"You're actually lucky—most people don't find out until they start breaking bones. What you have is more common in post-menopausal women. It's highly unusual for a 60-year-old male. We're going to need to do some more tests to see if there is something else going on."

I was shocked. I knew it ran in my family, but my bone density numbers were worse than my 86-year-old mother's. And as far as I knew, I was still very much pre-menopausal.

After two months of blood tests, urine tests, hormone tests, and specialist visits, they concluded it was due to some combination of genetics and not eating enough dairy. Perhaps I shouldn't have thrown that soft serve in the trash.

"Mr. Shea," said the doctor. "In addition to calcium and vitamin D supplements, we're going to put you on a synthetic hormone to build up your bones. You'll need to inject it every day for two years. After that, you'll take annual IV infusions of another medication to maintain the bone growth."

I was silent for a few moments. "Anything else?" I asked.

"You need to be really careful. For now you shouldn't be lifting more than ten to fifteen pounds. There's no way to tell how much weight your bones can handle before you have a fracture."

My granddaughter already weighed eighteen pounds. This was a gut punch.

"Also, you need to be doing weight bearing exercise every day, like walking or hiking. It will help your body build bone."

"What about biking?"

"Biking is not weight bearing. Neither is swimming. Biking can also be dangerous. You can't afford to fall."

"No biking?"

"Mr. Shea, your bones are very brittle right now. The risk of a fracture is very high."

I was crushed. What would I tell my granddaughter when she asked Pappy to pick her up? What would I tell Marty when he asked Jumbo to go for a bike ride?

"How about easy rail-trail stuff? If I take it slow?"

"You should be very cautious for the next two years, while

you're building back the bone. The risk will be lower after that, and you can get back to it. If you really want to bike now, if you're careful and don't fall, I suppose you can ride a little bit. But most of your exercise should be weight bearing."

Well, there it was. I'd been in perfect health my whole life. This was the first bad news I'd ever received. I honestly didn't know how to handle it.

As I drove home from the doctor's office, as is my habit, I started playing out all kinds of worst-case scenarios. Then I caught myself. I began thinking about the Camino.

I thought about the people we'd met who were facing real hardships. I thought about the words written on those stones at the Iron Cross and the pictures of lost loved ones. I thought about my stone, sitting where I'd left it, representing burdens yet to come (I guess that time was now). And I thought about the descent from that mountain, and how lucky I was that I didn't wreck while going 40 mph through those hairpin turns.

I told Katie and our sons, and then told Marty and Belle. They all helped me get some perspective on it. It wasn't cancer, or a heart attack, or anything life-threatening. Sure, I'd need to make some lifestyle adjustments for the next couple of years. But these were small things, and projected success rate of the treatment program was very high.

So, as I write this a year later, I'm taking my medicine. I'm a little more careful when walking down stairs or on an icy sidewalk. I sit with my granddaughter in my lap and play with her on the floor. I take Katie on trips we've always talked about, sometimes letting her lift my luggage for me. And I'm walking and hiking more than biking these days.

But make no mistake, I am still biking some. And a year from now, I plan on biking a lot more. I've decided "Get Up and Walk" doesn't have the same ring to it.

Marty and I will return!

AFTERWORD
BY MARTY

Jim and I are humbled that you have taken the time to read about and share in our Camino experience. We sincerely hope, as you turned the pages and followed our journey, that you felt as if you were along with us. In some ways, our whole time on the Camino seemed like we were reading a book. Each minute, each hour, and each day was a new page. We savored being immersed in the moment while looking toward what might be coming next. This is the magic, the gift the Camino presents. It's like a book you can't put down, a book written with lush detail of surroundings, truly amazing people, and life-changing adventures and awareness.

Jim took on the large task of describing the splendor that 1200 years of human history have contributed to the Camino. Rare is the moment when there is not something worthy of one's attention.

The Camino teems with natural and man-made beauty. The majestic landscapes of the meseta's seemingly endless plains disappear into the horizon. Villages scattered along the Camino's meandering path welcome pilgrims on their way to

Santiago. The cathedral towns on the Camino inspire with their testaments of faith, art, and history.

The collective energy and spirit that fills the air for its entire length is impossible not to pick up on and be elevated by when on the Camino. Every pedal stroke on our bikes was powered by these forces, and I'm not sure I ever felt more alive or invigorated deep down in my soul as I did during the days immersed in our ride. It is both humbling and empowering to submit to the spirit of the Camino, simultaneously rising and responding to the physical challenges it presents, while being reminded to live in and fully appreciate the moment as we pushed forward.

I say these things about the Camino in retrospect. As a long time cyclist, I began this journey simply thinking of it as an exciting bike ride, something a little different, but still just a bike ride. It gradually became more than that. When we arrived at the Iron Cross after a challenging climb and saw the mountain of mementos left by pilgrims who passed through here, my awareness of the spiritual element of the Camino reached its peak. Adding my own stone and private prayer, I truly felt the symbolism of leaving a burden behind and continuing on with a renewed spirit. I reflected on how much I love my wife and the family we have created together. At this moment my bike ride morphed into a pilgrimage, and the feeling stayed with me for the rest of the way to Santiago.

Jim and I are very close, and our pilgrimage is something we will share for the rest of our lives. As always happens when we are together, we experienced many moments of fun and laughter. We were also able to have our own private thoughts and reflections that the Camino so generously offered. Being able to have silent time with someone else is a testament of a genuine friendship!

Arriving in Santiago, we were greeted by an enormous crowd of pilgrims who had completed their own pilgrimages. I will always remember seeing thousands of people singing, dancing, and hugging—all celebrating together on that beautiful day. As time passes and many of the other memories experienced on the Camino begin to fade, this moment remains indelible.

Buen Camino!

ACKNOWLEDGMENTS

I grew up in a family of four children, with one older sister and two younger brothers. Our sister was an English major and loved to read books. The boys, not so much. Our mom would try to get my brothers and me to read, and we always resisted.

So you can imagine my mother's surprise when I told her I was writing the first "Get Up and Ride" book several years ago. When I handed her a draft and asked for her feedback, she said, "It's great, Jimmy. Since you never read books, you weren't influenced by great authors such as Steinbeck and Hemingway. It reads just like you talk—it's your *own style.*"

I thanked her for the back-handed compliment, then asked if she had any more specific comments. She handed me a printout of the entire draft, smothered in red ink. She was spot on with all her edits, and it helped turn my ramblings into an actual book.

When I told her I was working on a second book about our Camino trip, she was the first person I turned to for help. Now 86, my mom (Phyllis Shea) is one of the best writers I know. We sat down next to each other at her dining room table for an entire week, working through my draft page-by-page. Best of all, she made me dinner each evening, and we played music together each night. Thanks, Mom.

My acknowledgements wouldn't be complete without thanking another Phyllis—my sister, the English major, who was inside reading while I was outside playing baseball. All that reading paid off: her detailed edits were extremely helpful.

If you ever need an editor, I recommend using one named Phyllis. I know where you can find one (or two).

Marty's wife, Belle, was my partner in creating the first "Get Up and Ride" book, and she came through again on this one. She was the first to read my draft and give feedback, and she jumped in and worked her artistic magic in creating the maps. She also was our cheerleader before and during the ride, and she gave us the stones to place at the Iron Cross. Thanks Belle!

Marty and I would like to thank our dear friend, Pat Wood, who, along with his cousin, Dave, met us in Spain and treated us to two wonderful dinners, many laughs, and a memorable trip to Cape Finisterre. Thanks, Pat, you are like a brother to us.

I owe a debt of gratitude, not only for her editing, but for 36 years of wonderful marriage, to my wife, Katie. While I do enjoy biking with Marty, I prefer doing most other things with Katie (no offense, Marty). She supported me through the trip and the whole book-writing process, and her feedback on the book made the final product much better. Thanks, my love.

I mentioned in the chapter on "Reflections" that the Camino itself unexpectedly became a main character in this book. This centuries-old trail has seen everything—from wars and plagues to blisters and sprained ankles. But it has also seen healing, triumph, joy, and new relationships, some of which have even become marriages. All the while, it has provided a way for people of all ages and ethnic backgrounds to come together with a common mission—making it to Santiago. Thanks, Camino, we couldn't have done it without you.

Last, I am thankful for having a great friend in Marty. He supported me on our journey, keeping me positive and calm when I got frustrated, helping me with my bike, and always having the right perspective on the trip. "Jumbo, pinch yourself. We're riding our bikes in Spain!"

RESOURCES

Please review the book on Amazon or Goodreads—thank you!

All the photos in this book (and more!) can be seen in full color on our website: getupride.com. Sign up for our newsletter while you're there!

Follow us on Facebook! Facebook.com/GetUpandRideBook

Here are some Camino resources we found to be most helpful:

Guide Books:
Cycling the Camino de Santiago (Camino Francés), by Mike Wells
A Pilgrim's Guide to the Camino de Santiago, by John Brierley

Websites:
American Pilgrims on the Camino: Americanpilgrims.org
Camino Ways: Caminoways.com
Pilgrim's Reception Office in Santiago de Compostela: oficinadelperegrino.com

Facebook Groups:
BICIGRINOS, Camino De Santiago en Bicicleta: https://www.facebook.com/groups/bicigrino
Cycling - American Pilgrims on the Camino: https://www.facebook.com/groups/CyclingAmericanPilgrims

Bike Route Planning and Rentals:
Bicigrino: Bicigrino.com
Camino Ways: Caminoways.com
GPS tracks for the Camino: https://ridewithgps.com/routes/215419?lang=en

Accommodations:
Booking.com, Gronze.com, Airbnb.com

Baggage Shuttle Services:
Jacotrans (Jacotrans.es) or NCS (ncsequipajes.com)

Shipping bikes home, or buying a bike box in Santiago: Correos.es

ABOUT THE AUTHOR

Jim Shea is the author of the "Get Up and Ride" series of humorous true stories about his cycling adventures with his brother-in-law, Marty. Jim started writing books later in life after a forty-year career in technology sales and marketing. Originally from the Washington, DC area, Jim now lives in Pittsburgh, PA with his wife, Katie. They have three adult sons and are especially fond of their new role as grandparents.

Jim also plays acoustic guitar and sings folk, classic rock, and contemporary Christian music. He attended the University of Notre Dame (GO IRISH!) and Stanford University's Graduate School of Business.

Jim and Marty have cycled the Camino de Santiago, the Great Allegheny Passage/C&O Canal, and other epic trails. They are currently contemplating their next adventure.

ALSO BY JIM SHEA

GET UP AND RIDE
A STORY OF TWO FRIENDS AND A CYCLING ADVENTURE ON THE GREAT ALLEGHENY PASSAGE AND C&O CANAL

If you enjoyed the ride with Marty and Jim on the Camino, you'll love reading about their adventures on the Great Allegheny Passage (GAP) and C&O Canal!

In the summer of 2010, the pair embarked on a 335-mile cycling trip from Pittsburgh, Pennsylvania to Washington, DC. Chance encounters with colorful local characters and other escapades made for nonstop laughs.

As they rode through forests and along winding rivers, they experienced the breathtaking scenery of western Pennsylvania, Maryland and West Virginia, exploring early American history while learning more about each other as well as themselves.

Hold onto your handlebars—this is a side-splitting ride!

"An adventurous tale"
   - *Pittsburgh Post-Gazette*

"A true GAP/C&O trail experience with humor and history."
   - *Meyersdale Historical Society Visitor Center*

Available at Amazon, Barnes & Noble, and many local bookstores.

Made in the USA
Columbia, SC
21 June 2025

59686303R00174